THE
COLLEGE
PRESS
NIV
COMMENTARY

1, 2 & 3 JOHN

THE COLLEGE PRESS NIV COMMENTARY

1, 2 & 3 JOHN

MORRIS M. WOMACK

Volume Co-Editors:

Tony Ash, Ph.D.
Abilene Christian University

Kenny Boles, M.A.
Ozark Christian College

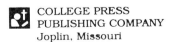
COLLEGE PRESS
PUBLISHING COMPANY
Joplin, Missouri

International Standard Book Number 0-89900-640-X

A WORD
FROM THE PUBLISHER

Years ago a movement was begun with the dream of uniting all Christians on the basis of a common purpose (world evangelism) under a common authority (The Word of God). The College Press NIV Commentary Series is a serious effort to join the scholarship of two branches of this unity movement so as to speak with one voice concerning the Word of God. Our desire is to provide a resource for your study of the New Testament that will benefit you whether you are preparing a Bible School lesson, a sermon, a college course or your own personal devotions. Today as we survey the wreckage of a broken world, we must turn again to the Lord and his Word, unite under his banner and communicate the life-giving message to those who are in desperate need. This is our purpose.

FOREWORD

It has been my pleasure to have been associated with Professor Morris Womack since the middle 1960s when we both accepted positions in the Los Angeles area with what was then Pepperdine College (now University). I have observed his growth as he developed into a distinguished and popular teacher, an accomplished author, diligent scholar, successful minister, and respected bishop of the church. He did these things while he maintained close, loving and productive ties with his family, friendship with his students, and exemplified a servant's attitude to those with whom he came in contact. Having demonstrated himself to be a man whose life in many ways illustrates that love which Christ said would identify his followers, I find it fitting that he should add this commentary on the three epistles of the "Apostle of Love" to his accomplishments.

As one peruses the pages of this work, it will be evident that the author has been able to balance his extensive theological training with his determination that this be a useful and practical work. While he shows mastery of the original language, the historical-cultural setting, the mechanics of biblical interpretation, and a profound acquaintance with the biblical text; he does so with an eye to clear exposition and insightful application of the basic issues portrayed by the Apostle John.

In his commentary on the biblical text, Professor Womack gives special attention to the developing problem of the gnostic heresy. The representatives of this aberrant religious group were dedicated to a view of Christ which in a very real sense robbed him of both his humanity and his divinity. In much the spirit of Athens, their prideful intellect displaced God and relegated to the trash heap of foolishness and naivete those who sought to follow his word. Considering themselves to be above sin, they heralded the virtues of thought and intellectual enterprise while belittling the ignorant folk who believed that following Christ meant obeying his teachings.

Dr. Womack points out that although John said these false teachers were no longer to be considered part of the fellowship (2:19), they considered the church to be their mission field (2:26, 3:7). It therefore is incumbent on church leaders to "mark heresy promoters and not allow them to bring division in the body." It was obviously not the position of the Apostle John that "I'm O.K. and you're O.K." regardless of religious belief. Eusebius claimed that Polycarp, a disciple of John, reported to Irenaeus that on one occasion when the apostle entered the baths at Ephesus and saw the gnostic leader, Cerinthus inside, he immediately left the baths saying, "Let us flee, lest also the baths fall in, since Cerinthus is inside, the enemy of the truth." It is those who obey Christ that by so doing prove that they know him, while those who claim to know him without submitting to his will only prove themselves to be liars (2:3-6).

However, it is especially in this emphasis upon John's insistence that Christians who claim to love God must also love one another that Professor Womack challenges the hypocrisy of a self-centered and legalistic spirit. The refinement of this "son of thunder" into the "Apostle of Love" is presented as both a challenge and a hope for all of us. Jerome reports that when in old age John had to be carried to the place of assembly, he always greeted the church with the words, "little children, love one another." When, perhaps somewhat impatiently, he was asked why he always said the same thing, he responded, "Because this is the Lord's command, and enough is done when this is done."

COLLEGE PRESS NIV COMMENTARY

I am honored to have the opportunity of recommending to you this faithful, and objective aid to your study and understanding of the words of the Holy Spirit as they were revealed through the Apostle John.

Carl Mitchell, Ph.D.
Professor of Bible & Religion
College of Bible & Religion
Harding University
Searcy, Arkansas

I would like to thank John Hunter, Dan Rees, and Saundra Tippett for their creative help. In the writing of 2 and 3 John, C. Michael Moss of Lipscomb University was gracious in allowing the editorial team to use material from a forthcoming book on John's epistles. A special thanks to Steve Cable and Chris DeWelt who have been a source of encouragement in the project.

I appreciate very much the kind words of Dr. Carl Mitchell of Harding University and for his support for the commentary that I have written. He is a friend and loyal brother.

Morris M. Womack

ABBREVIATIONS

INTRODUCTION

John's writings have been my favorite books of the Bible. This does not mean that they are more important than any others, but I like the spirit and tone as well as the content of his writings. They show how one can develop from a "son of thunder," as John was called by Jesus (Mark 3:17) to become the great apostle of love. His teachings on love are the deepest and most precious in the Bible. It was said early in church history (Jerome) that when John would come to the assembly of Christians, he would be carried to the door of the place of meeting where he would pat the Christians on the head, saying, "my little children, love one another."

The greatest memory I have about John comes from my freshman year in college when I began studying Greek. First John was the first place we began reading and translating. I remember it as a simple, clear, and challenging book. It was written in simple, unencumbered Greek, and this impression has stayed with me.

AUTHORSHIP[1]

These three epistles we are studying are referred to as "general epistles." They were not written to specific churches, as were the letters by the apostle Paul. While Jesus was on

---

[1]See the exemplary discussion of dating and authorship for Johannine writings in John A.T. Robinson, *Redating the New Testament* (Philadelphia: Westminster, 1976), pp. 254-311. He attests to the diverse range of scholars who agree on John's authorship.

earth, he selected three of his twelve disciples to be a sort of "inner circle." In his treatise on the life of Jesus, John referred to himself as "the disciple whom Jesus loved" (John 21:7). There are several indications of John's special relation to Jesus. He was one of the select three (Peter, James, and John) with Jesus at the transfiguration. He shared a lonely night in the Garden of Gethsemane prior to Jesus' trial and crucifixion, and he leaned on Jesus' breast and enjoyed a close encounter with Jesus at the last supper.

Some commentators prefer to separate the introductions to 1 John from one for 2 and 3 John. Given their differences, it is understandable to treat them accordingly. We will consider an overview of the three epistles together for this commentary. Traditionally, John the apostle has been accepted as the author of all three books but not without controversy over the centuries. First John is not structured like the typical first century letters and has *not* been called an epistle in the same light as both 2 and 3 John, which are very typical of early letter form and style. One of the greatest evidences for the books is that all three are found in the earliest Greek manuscripts. Irenaeus attributed authorship to John (*Against Heresies* III, 16, 5, and 8).

Internal evidence for the three letters point to the same author as that of the Gospel of John most credibly because of the claim of being an eye witness (1 John 1:1-3).[2] Language, key words, thought, scope and style are similar. A.E. Brooke in his commentary used the comparative work of John's first

---

[2]*The NIV Study Bible* suggests that "he may have been a first cousin of Jesus (his mother may have been Salome, possibly a sister of Mary; cf Mt 27:56; Mk 15:40; 16:1; Jn 19:25 — this view assumes that 'his mother's sister' in this verse refers to Salome; some further assume that 'Mary the wife of Clopas' in this verse stands in apposition to 'his mother's sister,' which would mean that this Mary and Salome were one and the same person" — Kenneth Barker, General Editor, *The NIV Study Bible* (Grand Rapids: Zondervan, 1995), p. 1904. The possibility of two "elders" living in Ephesus has not been successfully defended through time leaving John as the most likely author.

epistle with his Gospel by Holtzmann who wrote in 1882.[3] The comparison of phrases and terminology provide sufficient evidence to convince the honest seeker of John's authorship of the first epistle. If the commonality of the first epistle with the other two can be shown, the authorship problem is settled on John the apostle. (For example, 1 John 2:7 compares with 2 John 5 and John 13:34-35. Second John 12 compares with 1 John 1:4 and John 15:11; 16:24. The use of "my children" in 3 John compares with 1 John 2:1, etc.)

DATE AND OCCASION

All three letters can be safely dated at the end of the Apostle John's life. If this is accurate, it explains the brevity of 2 and 3 John especially since they would have been written by an old man. We are at a loss to discover from the letters themselves when and from where they were written. John had been exiled to the Isle of Patmos, as is stated in the book of Revelation. Whether John wrote these while he was on the Isle of Patmos, we do now know. It is most commonly thought that John wrote from Ephesus in the last decade (the middle of the 90s) of the first century[4] where John spent his last days.

One reason to handle all three books in one introduction is the fact that they share a common occasion with similar circumstances. Three major problems existed during this time: the spread of persecution by the Roman Empire, the development of false teachings of various kinds in the Christian community, and the rise and growth of Gnosticism. False prophets

---

[3]A.E. Brooke, *A Critical and Exegetical Commentary on the Johannine Epistles*, The International Critical Commentary (Edinburgh: T. & T. Clark, 1971), pp. ii-ix. Holtzmann compares the Greek text of both the similarities and the differences and peculiarities, such words as "life," "truth," "fellowship," and "the Spirit."

[4]Brooke Foss Westcott, *The Epistles of St. John* (London: Macmillan, 1883), p. xxxii.

or false teachers were attacking the church and that prompted the need for an authoritative response (see the section
below, *Gnosticism, Docetism*). John, as perhaps the last living
apostle at the time of writing, could speak with apostolic
authority from the Lord. Deceivers and antichrists were calling
to the sheep and the Lord sent John to shepherd God's flock.
All three situations were faced with the need to strengthen
fellowship among the true believers in order to recognize the
counterfeit gospel being preached. The heretics were unset-
tling the firm moorings of the gospel causing some to doubt
the first commands of Christ. Were they still loved by God?
What is truth? Who are the children of God? Can I have one
foot in heaven and also have one on earth? Did Jesus become
a man? How could he be divine too? Who is my neighbor and
how do I treat him? What if I do not feel saved? What if you
have a problem with a "ruling elder?" Diotrephes in 3 John
was wanting more authority. It is my view that this could well
be the beginning of a striving for power. Ignatius, in the early
second century, tells us of a bishop, elders, and deacons in
some early churches. The bishop seems to begin to take
power within the local church with the elders and deacons
working "under" him. These questions challenge the letter
writer for solid, inspired answers. John delivers!

Some commentators, such as Lenski and Marshall, have
suggested that 2 and 3 John may have been written first and
then 1 John. I simply mention this possibility and direct you
to these commentators for further discussion.

Why did John write these short letters? First John 5:13
specifically states the author's purpose in writing, "I write
these things to you who believe in the name of the Son of
God so that you may know that you have eternal life." The
theme of 2 John may be expressed in verse 9, "Anyone who
runs ahead and does not continue in the teaching of Christ
does not have God; whoever continues in the teaching has
both the Father and the Son." John summarizes the content

of 3 John in verse 11, "Dear friend, do not imitate what is evil but what is good. Anyone who does what is good is from God. Anyone who does what is evil has not seen God." Commentators vary in their opinions as to the epistles' key words and verses, but these will serve as one-verse representatives of their respective themes.

RECIPIENTS

It has been suggested that 1 John was a circular or an encyclical letter much like Paul's letter to the Ephesians. This is partially reasoned from the lack of an addressee. If both of these books were connected to Ephesus, they may have shared a similar tradition. If 2 and 3 John were also encyclical, they were intended to be passed around to various churches and individuals for all to read. All three of John's letters are sent to Christians.[5] Other than that we do not know who they were or where they lived. Area churches in Asia Minor (now Turkey) have been the most commonly proposed recipients. This opinion is based on the place of composition being Ephesus and that strikingly similar heresies are addressed, albeit incipient, in the earlier writings of the apostle Paul. John must have given much tender care and love to many of these churches in his last years around Ephesus. Based on Jesus' charging John to care for Mary at the time of the crucifixion, it is believed that Mary went home with John and spent her life at Ephesus. There is a traditional tomb of Mary in the ancient ruins of Ephesus today. John may have played an actual role in the founding and fostering of the church there.

---

[5]Everett F. Harrison, *Introduction to the New Testament* (Grand Rapids: Eerdmans, 1971), p. 447 — mentions the possibility that the readers of 1 John could be Gentiles based on 1 John 5:21 and the warning about idols.

GNOSTICISM, DOCETISM

What we face today in humanistic and New Age teachings we can identify as merely a refashioning of the old gnostic falsehoods. There is indeed nothing new under the sun! To understand the noxious weeds we fight today, we must turn back the pages of time to expose their beginning roots.

Whatever part John played in the birth and development of the Ephesian congregation, he was certainly involved in protecting them from the encroaching dangers of Gnosticism in the final years of the first century and following. As a witness to all of Jesus' personal ministry, John was quite capable of bearing witness to the historical Jesus and could certainly testify of the dual human/divine nature of Jesus Christ.

The rise and development of Gnosticism had a tremendous impact on the Christian movement. Around the middle of the first century, a monster in the form of Gnosticism arose that threatened the very roots of the Christian religion. The apostle Paul used the term ψευδωνύμου γνώσεως (*pseudōnymou gnōseōs*, "falsely-named knowledge") to identify this threat, Gnosticism (1 Tim 6:20). It presented a new worldview on the relationship between God and humanity which threatened Christianity at the time of its burgeoning growth.

Gnosticism, in my view, was a combination of three major strains of thought: Zoroastrianism, Platonism, and Christianity. Zoroastrianism, the religion of Persia, contributed at least two major elements: dualism (the worship of two gods) and the light-darkness views of Gnosticism (referred to in both John's Gospel and the Epistles of John). The dualism — the presence of two gods (a god of the Old Testament who created all things including evil and materialism and a god of the New Testament for the Gnostics whom they believed was the God of Jesus Christ) was expressed by Zoroastrianism by their two gods — Ahura Mazda (god of light) and Ahura Mainyu (god of darkness). The Jewish nation, having been exposed to the Persian religion during the Babylonian Captivity, were certainly influenced by this ideology.

Platonic and Neoplatonic philosophy contributed to the Gnostic theories through the concept of Plato's "world of ideas," which suggested that nothing exists except in an unseen world of ideas. The gods could not be approached or seen, said the Gnostic. God was at a distance from humankind, the Gnostics argued. In gnostic thought, humans could approach God through a series of "aeons" or "angelic" types of beings.

Some of the elements of Christianity found a welcome home among the Gnostics. The goodness of the God of the New Testament and the importance of knowing about God were some of these elements. The followers of the gnostic religion created a higher level of Christians, the gnostic Christians whom they regarded as the ultimate essence of their spiritual life.

John was not called one of the "sons of thunder" for nothing! Over the course of his lifetime he learned to direct his anger, or euphemistically called "righteous indignation," toward heretical causes aimed at the Christ. One of John's crucial reasons for writing was to answer the attacks by the false teachers faced by the recipients of all three letters.

Christians saw Gnosticism as a threat to the church as early as the last half of the first century. We can find some elements in some of Paul's writings and certainly in John's first epistle. When many biblical critics, especially the critics of the Tübingen school and others in America, began their critical analyses of the New Testament, they generally agreed that many of the New Testament books could not have been written in the first century because they reflected and even opposed the Gnostics, which they argued did not exist until the second century. At that time, many scholars argued that Gnosticism was a second-century phenomenon. I argued in the late 1950s that it originated much earlier. In fact, I wrote that "Until fairly recent times, scholars did not realize the vast span of history that Gnosticsim had. Though it was not called such, it can be traced to pre-Christian times."[6] This claim was questioned by some, but later research by more eminent scholars than I have supported this theory. William F. Albright, eminent paleontologist, had espoused the late authorship of several canonical books of the New Testament. However, near the end of his life he wrote, "all the New Testament books were probably written during the late forties and the early eighties of the first century A.D., possibly even between A.D. 50 and A.D. 75."[7]

The gnostic movement was a prominent influence on first century thought, very strong by the end of the century. That Gnosticism was prominent by the middle of the first century is further evidenced by the presence of the Nag Hammadi Manuscripts, gnostic documents discovered in the late 1940s. They are believed by some to have been nearly as old as the Dead Sea Scrolls. They are gnostic in character and must have been known by many of the period. Gnosticism was a dualistic religion (arguing for the existence of two opposing gods) and taught that Jesus was not really human but that Jesus was probably adopted by God at the time of his baptism (often referred to as the "Adoptionist Theory"). It was a divisive religion and was causing many problems in the early church.

Incipient Gnosticism[8] had been introduced in Colossians

---

[6]Morris Womack, "A Study of Heresies of the Second Century" (B.D. thesis, Butler University, 1958), p. 15.

[7]William F. Albright, "Retrospect and Prospect in New Testament Archaeology," in *The Teacher's Yoke: Studies in Memory of Henry Trantham*, E. Jerry Vardeman and James Leo Garrett, Jr., eds. (Waco, TX: Baylor University Press, 1964), p. 35.

[8]Gnosticism takes its meaning from the Greek word γνῶσις, *gnōsis* "knowledge." They taught that matter was totally evil and that spirit was totally good. Cult leaders were such men as Simon Magus (Acts 8), Valentinus, Basilides, Marcion and others. Later two extremes emerged: one that indulged the flesh (libertine) and one that denied the flesh (ascetic).

and somewhat in Corinthians.[9] John in his letters continues the battle he addressed in his Gospel, the battle most likely directed against "archheretic Cerinthus"[10] and his docetic followers.[11] One of the major concepts of the Christian gnostic movement was that Jesus was not born of human flesh, but that he only *seemed to be* human, hence the docetic philosophy. John had answered the docetic teaching that Jesus only "seemed" to be in the flesh[12] with his poetic Gospel opening. Later in 19:16-37, he explicitly describes the reality of Jesus' crucifixion.

The opening verses of 1 John clearly answered some of the heresy by giving an *eyewitness* account of knowing Jesus. As the popular saying goes, "been there, done that." John could say, "I have been there and seen Jesus do that." John also addressed the false belief "we have no sin" because they treated sin with indifference. And, there was no "special knowledge" or "special illumination" to be obtained by a few! Contrary to the false teachings, Jesus *did* come in the flesh and suffered and rose from the dead to give us life. John and those with him knew Jesus intimately. Jesus, Son of God, Creator of life, appointed John as an apostle with all the

---

[9]David Fiensy, *New Testament Introduction,* The College Press NIV Commentary (Joplin, MO: College Press, 1994, revised 1997), p. 297 — the Colossian description was of a more advanced Gnosticism than that possibly mentioned in 1 Corinthians. Also it is mentioned in 1, 2 Timothy, Titus and 2 Peter.

[10]Ibid., pp. 153-154, 352-353.

[11]Donald W. Burdick, *The Epistles of John* (Chicago: Moody, 1970), p. 13 — he believes in a more positive approach that 1 John was *not* specifically addressed to the Gnostics but to Christians. He does point out that Gnosticism was probably the most dangerous heresy facing the church in the first three centuries (p. 11).

[12]Docetism and docetics take their meaning from the Greek word δοκεῖν, *dokein,* "to seem." It has a long history and is difficult to specify any one teaching. See the helpful condensation of the topic in D.F. Wright, "Docetism," *Dictionary of the Later New Testament & Its Developments,* Ralph P. Martin & Peter H. Davids, eds. (Downers Grove: InterVarsity, 1997), pp. 306-309; a good summary of the main tenets of Gnosticism is given in *The NIV Study Bible,* p. 1905.

rights and authority given by God. Any commands are to come from God and not from man.

STRUCTURE AND STYLE

Alexander Ross organizes the main part of 1 John, apart from the preface and conclusion, under two main points: I. God Is Light (1 John 1:5–2:29), and II. God Is Love (1 John 3:1–5:12).[13] Robert Law outlined 1 John according to cycles of tests for truth and righteous living.[14] Regarding 2 and 3 John, virtually all commentators provide a simple outline for their brief contents.

J.W. Roberts offers a unique analysis of John's letters in relationship to his peculiar style. Among the ones Roberts[15] describes are John's use of "Antithetic Parallelism" (Hebrew device of contrasting two thoughts), "Genuine Antithesis" (or reverse of the same statement, as in 1 John 3:7-10), "Recapitulation" (as in 1 John 3:4a, repeating a word like "sin," "love," or "truth" and discussing it), "Word Parenthesis" ("inclusion of a thought unit between the first and last use of the same word" as in 1 John 5:16), and "Anaphora" (beginning with the same phrase like "If we say").

John's three letters have endeared themselves to the church since they were written in the first century. The original writer and the original audience have a much clearer view of things than we do. Were John's words heeded by his

[13]For one example of the two-point assessment see: Alexander Ross, *Commentary on the Epistles of James and John*, The New International Commentary on the New Testament (Grand Rapids: Eerdmans, 1970), p. 118.

[14]See Robert Law, *The Tests of Life: A Study of the First Epistle of St. John*, Third Edition (Grand Rapids: Baker, 1968), one of the best approaches to 1 John for treatment of the Christian disciplines and holy living.

[15]J.W. Roberts, *The Letters of John*, The Living Word Commentary, Everett Ferguson, ed.,Vol. 18, Second printing (Austin, TX: Sweet, 1969), pp. 13-15.

recipients? Obviously some did because the gospel message has continued through the preservation of the letters. As long as they are taught and preached, they will continue to instruct, warn, and encourage their readers. God bless you as *you* nobly search the Scriptures with the Lord Jesus.

BIBLIOGRAPHY

Arndt, William F. and F. Wilbur Gingrich. *A Greek-English Lexicon of the New Testament and Other Early Christian Literature*. Chicago and London: University of Chicago Press, 1979.

Barclay, William. *The Letters of John*. Philadelphia: Westminster, 1976.

Barker, Kenneth, Ed. *The NIV Study Bible*. Grand Rapids: Zondervan, 1995.

Brooke, A.E. *A Critical and Exegetical Commentary on the Johannine Epistles*. The International Critical Commentary. Edinburgh: T. & T. Clark, 1971.

Bruce, F.F. *The Epistles of John: Introduction, Exposition and Notes*. Grand Rapids: Eerdmans, 1970.

Burdick, Donald W. *The Epistles of John*. Chicago: Moody, 1970.

Burge, G.M. "John, Letters of." *Dictionary of the Later New Testament & Its Development*, pp. 587-599. Edited by Ralph P. Martin & Peter H. Davids. Downers Grove: InterVarsity, 1997.

Dodd, C.H. *The Johannine Epistles*. New York: Harper & Brothers, 1946.

Fiensy, David. *New Testament Introduction*. The College Press NIV Commentary. Joplin, MO: College Press, 1994. Revised 1997.

Harrison, Everett F. *Introduction to the New Testament*. Grand Rapids: Eerdmans, 1971.

Law, Robert. *The Tests of Life: A Study of the First Epistle of St. John*. 3rd ed. Grand Rapids: Baker, 1968.

Lenski, R.C.H. *The Interpretation of the Epistles of St. Peter, St. John and St. Jude*. Minneapolis: Augsburg, 1996.

Marshall, I. Howard. *The Epistles of John*. The New International Commentary of the New Testament. Edited by Ned B. Stonehouse, F.F. Bruce and Gordon D. Fee. Grand Rapids: Eerdmans, 1978.

McDowell, Edward A. *Hebrews-Revelation*. The Broadman Bible Commentary. Vol. 12. Nashville: Broadman, 1972.

Metzger, Bruce M. *A Textual Commentary on the Greek New Testament*. 3rd ed. New York: United Bible Societies, 1971.

Roberts, J.W. *The Letters of John*. The Living Word Commentary. Edited by Everett Ferguson. Vol. 18. 2nd printing. Austin, TX: Sweet, 1969.

Robinson, John A. T. *Redating the New Testament*. Philadelphia: Westminster, 1976.

Ross, Alexander. *Commentary on the Epistles of James and John*. The New International Commentary on the New Testament. Grand Rapids: Eerdmans, 1970.

Schaff, Phillip. *History of the Christian Church*. 8 vols. Grand Rapids: Eerdmans, 1950.

Smith, David. *The Expositor's Greek Testament*. Edited by W. Robertson Nicoll. 5 vols. New York: Hodder and Stoughton, 1922.

Smith, J.B. *Greek-English Concordance to the New Testament*. Scottdale, PA: Herald Press, 1955.

Staton, Knofel. *Thirteen Lessons on First, Second, and Third John.* Joplin: College Press, 1980.

Stott, John R.W. *The Letters of John: Introduction and Commentary.* Tyndale New Testament Commentaries. 1988. Reprint, Grand Rapids: Eerdmans, 1995.

Trench, Richard. *Synonyms of the New Testament.* Grand Rapids: Eerdmans, 1953.

Watson, D.F. "Rhetoric, Rhetorical Criticism," *Dictionary of the Later New Testament & Its Development*, pp. 1041-1051. Edited by Ralph P. Martin & Peter H. Davids. Downers Grove: InterVarsity, 1997.

Westcott, Brooke Foss. *The Epistles of St. John: The Greek Text with Notes and Essays.* London: Macmillan, 1883.

Wilkins, M.J. "Pastoral Theology," *Dictionary of the Later New Testament & Its Development*, pp. 876-882. Edited by Ralph P. Martin & Peter H. Davids. Downers Grove: InterVarsity, 1997.

Wright, D.F. "Docetism," *Dictionary of the Later New Testament & Its Development*, pp. 306-309. Edited by Ralph P. Martin & Peter H. Davids. Downers Grove: InterVarsity, 1997.

THE BOOK OF
1 JOHN

OUTLINE

1 JOHN 1

I. THE WORD OF LIFE (1:1-4)

[1]That which was from the beginning, which we[1] have heard, which we have seen with our eyes, which we have looked at and our hands have touched — this we proclaim concerning the Word of life. [2]The life appeared; we have seen it and testify to it, and we proclaim to you the eternal life, which was with the Father and has appeared to us. [3]We proclaim to you what we have seen and heard, so that you also may have fellowship with us. And our fellowship is with the Father and with his Son, Jesus Christ. [4]We write this to make our[a] joy complete.

[a]4 Some manuscripts *your*

The Greek text of these first four verses is actually only one sentence, which makes it a little more complicated for us in the English text. But John begins this epistle,[2] as well as his Gospel account, in much the same way as does the author of

---

[1]It is difficult, if not impossible, for us to know who "we" and "our" refer to in the five or six phrases in this chapter. Is John using the editorial "I" here, or is he referring to all of those who witnessed the events to which he refers? He may be thinking of Jesus' statement to the apostles in Acts 1:8, ". . . you will be my witnesses . . . ." I cannot say with certainty, but I tend to feel that he is using the expression to refer to all who heard and witnessed these grand events.

[2]Many who study this epistle regard it more as a treatise or sermon type of literature. It does not have the normal form of many of the ancient epistles. It also has the appearance of an encyclical, which was to be passed

33

Genesis: with an assumption. He assumes with great assurance that God exists. Genesis begins with the statement "In the beginning God . . . ." John merely asserts the presence of God; he feels no need to prove the existence of Deity. In his Gospel account, he stated, "In the beginning was the Word, and the Word was with God, and the Word was God" (John 1:1). Now he begins this first epistle with the same self-assured faith that God is. And no argument is needed! He does not try to prove that God is. God is! And that is that!

This was John's first proclamation concerning the bodily reality of the Son of God. It is the first of several attacks on the docetic teachers who, because they perceived themselves as spiritually advanced, were claiming that Jesus was never clothed with the physical attributes of humanity. He only *seemed* to be physical. He was not born, did not die, but He only *seemed* to. Since this epistle was written to assuage the fears and to build the faith of those who would read it in the light of the Gnostics' teaching about the bodily reality of Jesus[3], John begins his argument at the outset. John had seen, felt, and touched Jesus; he had talked to him, and had heard him speak. He could testify *personally* to Christ's reality. This *"Word of life"* about whom John wrote involves the message of Jesus, and he declares that he was a witness.

1:1 That which was from the beginning,

In this prologue to John's treatise, at least five major ideas stand out as major themes for the book. The first of these is *The Word was in the beginning*. It was the "Word" of God who actually brought creation into reality. God spoke, and it happened. John begins his epistle with this great

---

around for others to read. See the epistles of Paul for examples of the letter (or, epistle) form. Second and Third John are nearer the form of an epistle. Throughout this study, "epistle" will be used, but the reader should keep in mind this difference of opinions among various scholars.

[3]See the explanation of "Gnosticism" in the Introduction to this commentary.

truth: **That which was from the beginning.** He then identifies what was from the beginning as **the Word of life.** It was also the "eternal life, which was with the Father and has appeared to us." This phenomenal declaration has been identified with the beginning of all things. When one reads the fourth Gospel, it is easy to see the unity of John's entire message about the Christ. John opens the fourth Gospel with, "In the beginning was the Word [λόγος, *logos*, "word"], and the Word was with God, and the Word was God. He was with God in the beginning" (John 1:1,2). The same meaning is given to *logos* in 1 John as is given in the Gospel of John. John was not writing or speaking of something he had heard from others. He himself had seen, heard and touched Jesus.

At the time that John was writing, an early heretic by the name of Cerinthus also lived. He was a Gnostic who tried to explain the nature of Jesus in an altogether different way. He believed that Jesus was the Son of God, but he believed that Jesus was "adopted" by God sometime during Jesus' earthly life. This theory came to be known as the "Adoptionist Theory." Evidently, John was writing this treatise on the Word as a response to the false teachings of the Gnostics. Throughout this study, we will make reference to ideas that were gnostic in doctrine.

Jesus claimed to have been with God in the beginning. While praying his intercessory prayer, Jesus said "Father, glorify me in your presence with the glory I had with you before the world began" (John 17:5). If Jesus was not coeternal with God, he becomes the world's greatest liar. Either he is the Son of God, or he is an impostor.

which we have heard, which we have seen with our eyes, which we have looked at and our hands have touched — this we proclaim concerning the Word of life. 1:2 The life appeared; we have seen it and testify to it,

The second theme of the prologue is *The Word became flesh.*

35

The life appeared, John wrote.[4] It is a completed action. Elsewhere, John states that the "Word became flesh and made his dwelling among us" (John 1:14). God himself in the form of his Son Jesus actually lived among us as a man! John makes repeated emphasis on the factual reality of Jesus' life: he could be heard, seen, and touched. The Word indeed became flesh!

It was necessary for Jesus to become a man. The incarnation is one of the cardinal truths of Scripture. Without it, salvation would not be ours. From Adam forward, humankind has transgressed the law of God. Every last person has disappointed their Creator, the God of heaven. Something had to be done. A sacrifice needed to be offered. "[T]he law requires that nearly everything be cleansed with blood, and without the shedding of blood there is no forgiveness" (Heb 9:22). Christ became a man and offered himself "once for all[5] at the end of the ages to do away with sin by the sacrifice of himself" (Heb 9:23-36). It was necessary for Jesus to die. The apostle Paul wrote that Jesus needed to die so that he would be exalted (see Phil 3:7-8). Salvation could not be ours unless he died. The Docetists[6] maintained, however, that he only seemed to

---

[4] The expression, ἡ ζωὴ ἐφανερώθη, *hē zōē ephanerōthē*, "was made manifest," is an aorist passive form and this form signifies that it is an action already completed. Hence, the Word has already been made manifest.

[5] The expression "once for all" is a translation of ἅπαξ (*hapax*, "once") several times in the Scriptures. It signifies *once* in a given situation, not twice, but only once. That Paul was "stoned *once*" (2 Cor 11:25), "the priest went *once* a year" (Heb 9:7) and Christ was "*once for all* delivered to the saints" (Jude 3) are examples of the use of this word.

[6] The "Docetists" were those within the gnostic movement who did not believe in the incarnation of Jesus. I. Howard Marshall has the following comments that elucidated some of the concepts of Gnosticism: "Gnostic thinking was based on a sharp dualism between spirit and matter. The spiritual was regarded as divine and good, while the material was created and evil. It followed that the material world could not have been directly created by the supreme god, and different gnostic systems of thought devised various ways of explaining how the world had come into existence. One method was to postulate a series of beings or 'aeons' emanating from God and forming a long and complicated series, rather like a genealogical tree

COLLEGE PRESS NIV COMMENTARY

die. From the Greek word δοκέω (dokeō "it seems"), Docetism claimed that all that Jesus did that would be human — being born, eating, dying, etc. — only seemed to happen. Cerinthus, mentioned above, promoted this doctrine. Jesus was "adopted" by God at his baptism when the Spirit descended on him, or at some other time, and then only pretended to die on the cross. It was claimed that Simon of Cyrene not only carried the cross for Jesus, but he also was crucified in the place of Jesus while Jesus was watching and laughing from nearby (see the footnote by Marshall at the previously cited reference). A number of references in 1 John will show the impact of this false teaching.

and we proclaim to you the eternal life, which was with the Father and has appeared to us.
The third theme of this prologue is *Jesus is with us now and forever*. As he was about to ascend into heaven, he promised his disciples, "I am with you always" (Matt 28:20). On another occasion Jesus said, "[W]here two or three come together in my name, there am I with them" (Matt 18:20). Jesus is alive and with us.

We can be thankful that Christ brought us the greatest way of life one could conceive. Christianity is unique among all major world religions: it is the only religion with a *living* leader. No other world religion can make that claim. All the other leaders have been dead for centuries, but the religion Jesus brought did not even begin until he had died and was

---

turned upside down, so that God is at the top and successive groups of aeons occupy different, lower levels, until at last one of the aeons farthest away from God creates the world. By this means God could be relieved of responsibility for creating the world. But if God could not create the world, neither could he, nor his immediate relations, be united with the evil, material world in any real or lasting sort of way." (I. Howard Marshall, *The Epistles of John*, New International Commentary of the New Testament, Ned B. Stonehouse, F.F. Bruce and Gordon D. Fee, eds. [Grand Rapids: Eerdmans, 1978], p. 17.)

risen from the dead. His resurrection is the central fact of Christianity. John stresses the eternality of Jesus. He is so positive about this that he refers to Jesus' coming into the world this way: "The life appeared; we have seen it and testify to it."

1:3 We proclaim to you what we have seen and heard, so that you also may have fellowship with us. And our fellowship is with the Father and with his Son, Jesus Christ.

The fourth major theme of the prologue is *We have fellowship with the Father and the Son.* John declares that this proclamation of eternal life is being made **so that you may have fellowship with us. And our fellowship is with the Father and with his Son, Jesus Christ."** "Fellowship" is a very important word in the New Testament. It is translated from κοινωνία (*koinōnia,* "to have in common") and is involved in many aspects of the Christian life. It is used in the New Testament to refer to sharing with or helping someone in some common goal (see Acts 2:42); giving someone the "right hand of fellowship" (Gal 2:9); having a "oneness" in someone's suffering (Phil 3:10), to name a few of the uses. It is also used in Acts 2:42 to refer to interpersonal and interspiritual relationships within the church. The early Christians "devoted themselves to the apostles' teaching and to the fellowship . . ." (Acts 2:42). And John makes reference in these verses to the "fellowship" which we have with God, with Christ, with the Holy Spirit and with each other.

It was especially important for John that our fellowship continue. False teaching and division tend to weaken or destroy the fellowship of the body. It appears to us that John views the role of fellowship as extremely vital. Although he uses the word *koinōnia* four times in this chapter, he is careful to show the interrelation between God and his Son with each other and with all of us. It is highly possible that John is emphasizing fellowship with God and his Son Jesus Christ to further stress the dangers of minimizing the incarnation as the Docetists were doing. Our fellowship is not with God only or Jesus only, but with *both* God and Jesus, as well as with all of the saints though the generations.

The early Christians often practiced what was referred to as "love feasts," or "agape feasts." These love feasts provided an opportunity for the new and inexperienced Christians to build strength from fellowship with other Christians in order to be able to cope with the world. Newborn Christians will seek out associations, and if these associations are not provided in the church, they will seek for them outside the family of believers. There is a constant need of fellowship, or love feasts, to provide support and love for each other.

With blessings, there come responsibilities. Fellowship is a great blessing, and has its attendant obligations. At least four of these were stressed by the early church. First, *a need to develop a mutual care for one another.* The most common word for Christian "love" in the New Testament is ἀγάπη (*agapē*, "love"). *Agapē* does not mean the same thing as friendship love nor does it necessarily develop mutuality. *Agapē* can be commanded, for it involves thinking of others in terms of considering their best interests. Paul suggested this form of love when he wrote, "Each of you should look not only to your own interests, but also to the interests of others" (Phil 2:4).

Second, *we should seek the presence of our brothers and sisters in the Lord.* The early Christians sought the "fellowship" of their fellow Christians. We tend to become like those who are significant to us. If we constantly seek the presence of those who are spiritually minded, we will tend to develop more spirituality ourselves.

Third, *we should share with those who have need.* The Parable of the Good Samaritan is an excellent illustration of how to serve those who have need (see Luke 10:25-37). Later in this epistle, John wrote, "If anyone has material possessions and sees his brother in need but has no pity on him, how can the love [ἀγάπη] of God be in him?" (1 John 3:17).

Fourth, *we have partnership in God's service*. What an exalt-ing thought! To literally have fellowship with the Creator of everything. God is my partner! Paul refers to the Philippians' "partnership [*koinōnia*] in the gospel from the first day until now" (Phil 1:5). They were partners because they shared with him in the work of preaching.

When we walk in the Light, and when we truly have the fellowship with God through his Son, we will have our sinful lives purified from all sin. We will live in a "purified-from-sin" relationship. We can constantly live in the presence of the Most High God. We can live in the shadow of the cross if we are willing to submit to the love of Jesus. What a highly favored people we are!

The fifth major theme of this prelude is *The Word will abide forever*. In other words, it is the Eternal Word. The expression "Word of God" should not be limited to the writ-ten word, or what we call the Bible. The living Word is Jesus Christ and he sent the Spirit to reveal to us the written word (see John 14:26). This Word is the living Word of God, the Son of God, and his revelation of salvation sent to us.

Christ is truly eternal. He died on the cross never to die again. He paved the way for all of those who believe on him so that they may never die. Death for the Christian becomes nothing more than a changing of worlds. We experience physical death, but, in truth, we have eternal life abiding in us already, because "Jesus lives forever" and intercedes for us to the Father (Heb 7:24- 25). Our future is secure; our hope is eternal. We believe in the Son of God who lives forever — the Eternal Word of God. In several places in this epistle, John assures us that eternal life is a here and now possibility, not a then and there. We have life *now* (see 1 John 5:11-13).

1:4 We write this to make our joy complete.

John ends the prologue with an interesting, if somewhat vague, statement. **We write this to make our joy complete.**

John uses the expression "I write unto you" at least eleven times in this epistle and twice in the negative, "I am not writing . . . ." He is very careful to inform his readers that he has specific reasons for writing to them. This brief sentence is a little difficult to understand completely. Some translations read "to make *our* joy complete," while other translations read "to make *your* joy complete."[7] If the correct translation is "our joy," then John is either speaking of his own joy (with an editorial use of "we") or a shared joy; if it is translated "your joy," then John is speaking about the joy of the recipients of the letter. I am prone to agree with the rendering of the American Standard Version, Revised Standard Version and New International Version which use the pronoun "our." Probably, in view of the discussion about the fellowship with God, Christ, and each other, the "complete" joy refers to how this great revelation of the Word to us affects all of us.

II. LIFE WITH GOD AND THE WORLD (1:5–2:27)

A. THE WAY OF LIGHT AND DARKNESS (1:5-7)

[5]This is the message we have heard from him and declare to you: God is light; in him there is no darkness at all. [6]If we claim to have fellowship with him yet walk in the darkness, we lie and do not live by the truth. [7]But if we walk in the light, as he is in the light, we have fellowship with one another, and the blood of Jesus, his Son, purifies us from all[a] sin.

[a]7 Or *every*

---

[7]The word for "our" is ἡμῶν (*hēmōn*, "our") while the word for "your" is ὑμῶν (*hymōn*, "your"). The two words are almost identical, except for the two initial vowels, *eta* and *upsilon*, each with a "rough breathing" transliterated as "h." Some ancient manuscripts use the first word while other manuscripts use the second. There is no way to determine which is correct, as both make equal sense in context.

1:5 This is the message we have heard from him and declare to you:

John is beginning to discuss some of the problems that the church is facing, mainly those associated with the gnostic movement. Having identified Jesus as the witnessed one who is the Word of God, he makes sure that his readers know that the message he is giving to them does not come from him, but from the "witnessed one," Jesus the Word. John R.W. Stott states that "[t]he link between this paragraph and the foregoing preface is in the word *message*. John has already used the verb a*pangellomen* ('we proclaim', v. 3); he now uses the very similar *anangellomen, we . . . declare*, in conjunction with the noun *angelia, message*. This message has not been invented by himself or the other apostles, but is what they *have heard from him*."[8] Through the Holy Spirit, John and the other apostles, Jesus the Word has given the readers the message as he promised he would (see John 14:26).

God is light; in him there is no darkness at all.

The message that John declared to them was, **God is light; in him there is no darkness at all**. The concept of light versus darkness in a religious sense is not new to the Christian era. The prophets of old recognized that God is light. The Psalmist wrote, "The LORD is my light and my salvation" (Ps 27:1). Isaiah wrote, "Your sun will never set again, and your moon will wane no more; the LORD will be your everlasting light, and your days of sorrow will end" (Isa 60:20). The "light-darkness" motif was very prominent in the Persian Zoroastrian religion. Their two gods — Ahura Mazda (the god of light, standing for their god of good, also called Ormazd) and Ahura Mainyu (the god of darkness, standing for their god of evil, also called Ahriman) — form the basis for the

---

[8]John R.W. Stott, *The Letters of John: Introduction and Commentary*, Tyndale New Testament Commentaries, (Grand Rapids: Eerdmans, 1988 and 1995), p. 75.

dualistic religious concept. In the Qumran community of the Essenes, there were documents centered around the concept of light and darkness. There was one document entitled *The War of the Sons of Light and the Sons of Darkness*. Just the mention of the title of this scroll emphasizes the importance of the "Light-Darkness" concepts of the early Christian world.

Light and darkness are also used by Jesus Christ and later by his inspired writers, like John in this reference. John wrote, "This is the message we have from him and declare to you: God is light; in him there is no darkness at all." Jesus was quoted by John as saying, "I am the light of the world. Whoever follows me will never walk in darkness, but will have the light of life" (John 8:12). Again, Jesus states that his followers are "the light of the world" (Matt 5:14). Jesus makes it clear that God is total light; no darkness is in him. Light, then, is God's representation of good; dark is God's symbol for evil. John states that "God is light, and there is no darkness in him." Not only is God light, but he is the source of all light; he spoke light into existence in the beginning (see Genesis 1:3). The Christians to whom John was writing were encouraged to "walk in the light;" we actually lie if we pretend to be God's children and "walk in darkness."

1:6 If we claim to have fellowship with him yet walk in the darkness, we lie and do not live by the truth.

In the next two verses, John connects all of this: the message, fellowship, living in the light, and our purification from sin. Those false teachers who "went out from us" (2:19) were "trying to lead you astray" (2:26) causing these Christians deep trouble and turmoil. John is beginning his warning of what they must do to protect their souls from being tainted by these false teachings.

1:7 But if we walk in the light, as he is in the light,

This statement is a little difficult to understand. Jesus *is* the light, but John uses the expression, "he is in the light."

Stott wrote, "God is eternally and necessarily in the light because he *is* himself light; we are called to walk in the light. God is in the light because he is always true to himself and his activity is consistent with his nature."[9] The very concept of God being the ultimate light is beyond our human comprehension; but, I believe the explanation Stott gives sheds light on what John was telling us.

we have fellowship with one another, and the blood of Jesus, his Son, purifies us from all sin.

The **blood of Jesus, his Son** would be repulsive to those who had separated themselves from those faithful to the incarnation of Jesus. The blood was a part of the incarnation, and this was physical and thus denied by those of the apostasy. The Gnostics, and especially the Docetists,[10] would deny that blood would have anything to do with salvation. F.F. Bruce wrote, "Most serious of all the consequences of their apostasy is this: the blood of Jesus, which is constantly accessible for the cleansing of those who remain within the fellowship, is not available for those who show a persistent preference for 'walking in darkness.'"[11] John connects the message, fellowship, living in the light, and purification from our sins together.

B. ADMITTING OUR SIN (1:8-10)

[8]**If we claim to be without sin, we deceive ourselves and the truth is not in us. [9]If we confess our sins, he is faithful and just and will forgive us our sins and purify us from all**

---

[9]Stott, *The Letters of John*, p. 80.

[10]The Docetists, as we have seen earlier, were those who promoted the idea that Jesus did not die, nor was he actually put on the cross. It only seemed that he died. Anything that identified Jesus with humanity was denied as only something that "seemed" to be true.

[11]F.F. Bruce, *The Epistles of John: Introduction, Exposition and Notes* (Grand Rapids: Eerdmans, 1970), p. 43.

unrighteousness. [10]If we claim we have not sinned, we make him out to be a liar and his word has no place in our lives).

[a]2 Or *He is the one who turns aside God's wrath, taking away our sins, and not only ours but also*

John is here attacking one of the central beliefs of the Gnostics: that real Christians do not sin. Bruce wrote, "These new teachers [those who went out from the Christians to whom John refers in 2:19] claimed to have reached such an advanced stage in spiritual experience that they were 'beyond good and evil.' They maintained that they had no sin, not in the sense that they had attained moral perfection but in the sense that what might be sin for people at a less mature stage of inner development was no longer sin for the completely 'spiritual' man."[12] This becomes a very damnable doctrine, for it led some early Christians to live licentious lives, because they believed they would not be punished for it.

1:8 If we claim to be without sin, we deceive ourselves and the truth is not in us.

Elsewhere in God's revelation we are told that there is no one who has not sinned except Jesus (Rom 3:23). These false teachers had undoubtedly convinced themselves that when one has the higher knowledge through their gnostic[13] characteristics, they were above sin. Sin was physical and involved an abuse of the physical body. John tells them that this is a lie.

Some commentators have difficulty with the statement "if we claim to be without sin" in verse 8 and the statement in verse 10, "If we claim we have not sinned." Is there some

---

[12]Bruce, *The Epistles of John*, p. 26.

[13]The word γνῶσις (*gnōsis*, "knowledge") from which we get the word "Gnostic," as the definition shows, means "knowledge." Those who held to this false teaching believed that God had given them a higher level of knowledge. Hence, their spiritual beings were on a higher level than other Christians. In fact, they saw the world divided into three types of people: Gnostics, ordinary Christians, and the unsaved.

difference between these two statements in the mind of John? John is saying that we ought not to claim we have no sins (present tense), and then we ought not to deny that we have had past sins. In either case — denial of present sin or denial of any past sins — we make God out to be a liar. J.W. Roberts stated that "in the first passage [v. 8] John refers to the sinful state; we must not argue that we are above sin so that no taint of its ugliness and stain may be found with us. Here [in v. 10] **have not sinned** refers to the committing of particular sins or deeds of unrighteousness."[14]

Those who were promoting these false teachings regarding having no sin, John represents as sinners. They were not only deceiving themselves, but they were deceiving those who believed what they were teaching. John also taught that those of us who claim that we have not sinned call God a liar; but we also "deceive ourselves and the truth is not in us." John is saying here that if we do not admit that we are sinners, the truth is not in us. In John's Gospel, he quotes Jesus as saying that, "I am the way and the truth and the life" (John 14:6). If the truth is not in us, then Jesus is not in us, for he is the truth.

1:9 If we confess our sins, he is faithful and just and will forgive us our sins and purify us from all unrighteousness.

Sin causes us to be guilty in the sight of God, therefore in need of forgiveness. John is writing to those who have been born again, or have been baptized. The requirement of confessing our sins does not invalidate other requirements that God has given for receiving forgiveness of sins (see Acts 2:38). Forgiveness is the result of God's unlimited love for us. The sin that makes us guilty in God's sight also makes us unclean, for sin not only defiles the body but also the spirit. So, when we are forgiven, we are also purified from all of the iniquities

---

[14]J.W. Roberts, *The Letters of John,* The Living Word Commentary, Vol. 18 (Austin, TX: Sweet, 1968), pp. 34-35.

which stain the soul and spirit. There is a wonderful power in the blood of Jesus Christ.[15]

1:10 If we claim we have not sinned, we make him out to be a liar and his word has no place in our lives.

John makes one more charge to those who would minimize the power of sin. Here, **have not sinned** likely refers to having committed specific sins. If we claim that we have not committed specific sins, we make **him out to be a liar**. Hence, this eternal "Word" which John has stressed cannot live in one who claims to have not sinned. Bruce wrote that the statement **his word has no place in our lives** is a much stronger statement than "his truth is not in us" (verse 8). Whatever the case, John is insisting that the false teachers are leading the faithful away from God and must be rejected.

---

[15]"Blood," specifically the blood of Jesus, is involved in our salvation. Throughout the Bible is the continuous theme of salvation through the blood of Jesus Christ. A few years ago, one of the major Christian denominations, in their ruling council, voted to delete the concept of blood from their hymnals, creedal statements, and other official documents. They reported that the reason they did this was because blood was repulsive to many people. They evidently forgot that blood has always had a significant place in religion.

God has always required a blood sacrifice. Do you remember that Abel offered a blood sacrifice to God? When Noah departed from the ark, he offered a blood sacrifice to God. The Hebrew writer declared that "the law requires that nearly everything be cleansed with blood, and without the shedding of blood there is no forgiveness" (Heb 9:22). Blood, namely the blood of Jesus which was shed at the cross, is central to salvation. John wrote that "the blood of Jesus, his Son, purifies us from all sin" (1 John 1:7). Jesus offered his sacrifice only once (see Heb 9:26).

1 JOHN 2

C. THE ATONING SACRIFICE (2:1-2)

[1]My dear children, I write this to you so that you will not sin. But if anybody does sin, we have one who speaks to the Father in our defense — Jesus Christ, the Righteous One. He is the atoning sacrifice for our sins, and not only for ours but also for[a] the sins of the whole world.

[a]2 Or *He is the one who turns aside God's wrath, taking away our sins, and not only ours but also*

2:1 My dear children, I write this to you so that you will not sin.

John probably uses the word τεκνίον (*teknion,* "little child") to indicate the vulnerability of these Christians due to their lack of mature experience in the Church. John, the disciple of love, was very fond of those to whom he was writing. He uses two intimately personal terms to refer to them: "my little children," or "dear children," and "dear friends."[1] It is interesting that this man whom Jesus called a "son of thunder" in his early days of discipleship would become by the end of his life the "disciple of love." This is a further evidence of the power of Jesus on one's life. This statement is another one of those places in

---

[1]Phillip Schaff wrote, "Jerome pictures him [John] as the disciple of love, who in his extreme old age was carried to the meeting-place on the arms of his disciples, and repeated again and again the exhortation, 'Little children love one another,' adding 'This is the Lord's command, and if this alone be done, it is enough.' This, of all the traditions of John, is the most credible and the most useful [tradition]." Phillip Schaff, *History of the Christian Church* (Grand Rapids: Eerdmans, 1950), I:430.

which John says, "I write to you so that . . . ." His purpose for writing was "that you will not sin." This is a continuation of the argument he has been making about his case against sin. Probably it would have been better if chapter 1 had been extended through 2:2, for he is discussing the same matter.

But if anybody does sin, we have one who speaks to the Father in our defense — Jesus Christ, the Righteous One. 2:2 He is the atoning sacrifice for our sins, and not only for ours but also for the sins of the whole world.
In 1 John 2:1-2, John is expounding on the remedy for sin. For, **if anybody does sin**, we have a remedy. If anyone sins, John says we have **one who speaks . . . in our defense.**[2] He identifies **Jesus Christ, the Righteous** as that one who speaks in our defense. He is "representing our case" before the Father as he promised he would do. He is, therefore, our defense attorney, and he will represent us to God not only as we ask for forgiveness, but also when we stand before him on the day of judgment. He is qualified to do this because he is the **atoning sacrifice for our sins.**[3] He has offered himself on the cross for our sins, and he has paid the debt for our guilt in the presence of God. This was the *atoning sacrifice* for our sins — but, not only for "our sins" but for the sins of all the world. John is not declaring here that this atoning sacrifice *unconditionally* paid the debt for out sins. We must *accept* the payment, obey his word and loyally serve him as our Savior.

---

[2]The word here is παράκλητον (*paraklēton*, "an advocate, intercessor,." one who is called alongside of. The word would also allow us to use "an attorney" who speaks in behalf of us.

[3]Ἱλασμός (*hilasmos*, "atonement, propitiation") has been translated with a number of words. The RSV uses "expiation"; the KJV and ASV both use "propitiation." The word "propitiation" was often used in ancient Greek to refer to "propitiating" or appeasing the anger of the gods. Even though Jesus' blood does "appease" the anger of God toward us because of our sins, it is my feeling that the NIV has a very acceptable translation, "our atoning sacrifice." God is not the merciless God in comparison to pagan gods. Our God is a loving and merciful God who is willing and able to forgive us. Jesus, his Son, sacrificed his body for our forgiveness.

D. KEEPING GOD'S COMMANDMENTS (2:3-6)

[3]We know that we have come to know him if we obey his commands. [4]The man who says, "I know him," but does not do what he commands is a liar, and the truth is not in him. [5]But if anyone obeys his word, God's love[a] is truly made complete in him. This is how we know we are in him: [6]Whoever claims to live in him must walk as Jesus did.

[a]5 Or *word, love for God*

It is evident that John is continuing his argument for acceptance of the "witnessed one," Jesus. John has presented Jesus to us as the one who was the eternal "Word of life," the life that appeared, with whom we have fellowship, the one who "speaks to the Father in our defense," and the one who is our "atoning sacrifice."

Coming to know Jesus involved developing an intimate relationship with him. The Greek word translated by the Eng;lish words "to know" is the same word used for a husband to know his wife intimately. Certainly John is not suggesting any kind of sexual connotation, but "to know" Jesus involves becoming one with him spiritually as a man becomes one with his wife physically. At this point, John presents Jesus as the one whom we are to obey. Those who had gone out from them, the false teachers, could admit to none of these characteristics, or qualities.

2:3 We know that we have come to know him if we obey his commands.

Does it seem incidental that John uses the word from which "Gnostic"[4] comes to indicate that "We know"? **We know** that we know him if we are obedient to his commands. John uses

---

[4]"Gnostic" comes from the Greek word γνῶσις (*gnōsis*, "knowledge"), and γνῶσις is the noun form of γινώσκω (*ginōskō*, "I know"). There were other words for knowledge, or knowing, that John could have used.

the perfect indicative to express "We have come to know him."[5] This expression was a challenge to the Gnostics to reckon with the implications of their false teachings. Their teachings make it impossible for their followers to accept a central foundation principle of Christianity; namely, the incarnation of Jesus. The Greek idea of knowledge was that it was an activity of the mind; but the Gnostics believed this special knowledge (γνῶσις, *gnōsis*, "knowledge") that they possessed was "a gift of God to man. It comes by revelation. The early church believed that that revelation began with Jesus and was handed down through the apostles and inspired teachers."[6]

So far in this epistle, John has testified to his own witness of Jesus' humanity (see 1:1-4). Now he is saying that we not only must believe in his humanity because there were witnesses to both his divine as well as his human existence, but we must also obey his commands. John suggests that Jesus added another dimension to this obedience, which is recorded in the Gospel account: "Whoever has my commands and obeys them, he is the one who loves me" (John 14:21). And, again, "If anyone loves me, he will obey my teaching. My Father will love him, and we will come to him and make our home with him. He who does not love me will not obey my teaching" (John 14:23-24). John asserts in this epistle that "if anyone obeys his word, God's love is truly made complete in him" (v. 5).

2:4 The man who says, "I know him," but does not do what he commands is a liar, and the truth is not in him.

This is a very strong indictment. Not only is such a person a liar, but the truth is not in him. This statement answers a question that many Christians have: "How can I know that I am a Christian?" John says that we come to know him when

---

[5]The verb here is ἐγνώκαμεν (*egnōkamen*, "we have known"), the perfect, active, 1st person plural of γινώσκω, which indicates an action that has already been completed: "we have already come to know him."

[6]Roberts, *The Letters of John*, VIII, p. 41.

we obey his commands. John's readers in the first century and we in this present century can know of a surety that we are children of God: if we have obeyed Jesus' commands, then "God's love is truly made complete in" us (v. 5).

2:5 But if anyone obeys his word, God's love is truly made complete in him. This is how we know we are in him:
The Gnostics held that they had to have had some supernatural outpouring of *gnōsis* ("knowledge") from God. The early Christians to whom John wrote had not experienced this outpouring, and they must have wondered what their relationship to God was. John states here that **God's love is truly made complete in him.** In the next short section, we will discuss more in detail this "love of God" which John identifies as "a new command."

2:6 Whoever claims to live in him must walk as Jesus did.
John has already stated that to have fellowship with God, we must walk in the light and Jesus *is* the light. One of the characteristics of John's writing style is that he often makes one point and then he states the concept in a negative form. For example, we come to *know him* if we obey his commandments; if we do not obey them, we are liars. Or, "God is light" and in him is no darkness. John uses some of the same analogies that Paul used. John sees our *being* "in him" and *living* "in him" as the same thing. So if we **live in him,** we must **walk as Jesus** walked. Jesus left an example that we should walk "in his steps" (see 1 Pet 2:21). Again, John may be striking at the gnostic docetic philosophy (the notion that Jesus only *seemed* to be human) when he refers to walking "as Jesus walked." Walking as Jesus walked, however, does not refer to some ritualistic religion; it is more than simply living a "form of religion"; it means truly walking an unselfish, God-centered life in all we do. Jesus was not interested in mere ritual and form; he was interested in our lives being God-like in all we do.

E. A NEW COMMANDMENT (2:7-8)

⁷Dear friends, I am not writing you a new command but an old one, which you have had since the beginning. This old command is the message you have heard. ⁸Yet I am writing you a new command; its truth is seen in him and you, because the darkness is passing and the true light is already shining.

This discussion of the "new command" and the "old command" is, in reality, a continuation of the previous paragraph; however, we are discussing it here as a new paragraph.

2:7 Dear friends,

John begins this discussion by referring to these Christians as ἀδελφοί (*adelphoi*, "brothers"). This word has been translated variously as "dear friends" (NIV), "brethren" (KJV), and "beloved" (RSV), to list a few. Literally the word is "brothers" or "brethren." Some of these other renditions are undoubtedly used to show the very close relationship John sustained with them, and I think with good intent. Certainly no harm is done to the language by showing this friendship relation. However, we should keep in mind that John was using language that indicated a family relationship, with God as Father.

I am not writing you a new command but an old one, which you have had since the beginning.

This is both **a new command** and **an old** command. John may be indirectly referring to a statement made by Jesus as recorded in his Gospel. "A new command I give you: Love one another. As I have loved you, so you must love one another. By this all men will know that you are my disciples, if you love one another" (John 13:34-35). Notice here that John has switched from the plural [commands, v. 3] to the singular [command]. In the light of John 13:34-35. it is easy to conclude that all of the commandments are summed up in one, namely, "to love one another." Jesus designated love as the identification mark of his disciples. There is no other command or practice anywhere else in Holy Scripture that so succinctly sums up the identification of Jesus' disciples.

It was a "new" command when Jesus first gave it. Love from Jesus' perspective was summarized in the word ἀγάπη (*agapē*, "love").[7] There are several Greek words that can be translated by our English word "love," but this use of love is a stronger form of love. It was rarely used in pagan or secular sources. Jesus uses the imperative mood (ἀγαπᾶτε, *agapate*). But the force of John's use of this imperative is that it is a strong "recommendation" or order to do so. If we want to obey the "new" command, we are *expected* to love one another. Some of the words used in the New Testament for "love" are more emotional in quality than *agapē* is. See the discussion of *agapē* and φίλος (*philos*) in the next paragraph. To love one another is to expect or desire that they be treated well.

This old command is the message you have heard.

But why does John refer to a *new* commandment, then says it is an *old* commandment? This command **is the message you have heard.** John calls this an old commandment because these Christians had known it "from the beginning." Beginning does not refer to the beginning of time, but the beginning of the gospel age, or at least the beginning of their acquaintance with the gospel. "Love" (or *agapē* as opposed to *philos* ["friendship love"]) had been a part of the message heard from the beginning (v. 5). So, it was an old message to

---

[7]Richard Trench, in his *Synonyms of the New Testament*, compares the two verbs ἀγαπάω and φιλέω. He suggests that the first is more an intellectual approach while the latter is more of an emotional approach to love. The former can be commanded; it is a healthy good will to others, or thinking of the best for them, while the latter stresses the emotional qualities. We are to will the best for even our enemies ("love your enemies," said Jesus). Some have suggested that we can love others without necessarily liking them. See Richard Trench, *Synonyms of the New Testament* (Grand Rapids: Eerdmans, 1953), pp. 41-44.

those who had heard it, but a new message to those who had not heard it before. When Jesus told his disciples of the "new command," it really was a new one. The word *agapē* had not been used in the same way or with the same meaning Jesus place upon it. It was a *new* message. It suggests a type of love than can be commanded. The other words for "love" connote a more emotional type of feeling. The new message was one of an unselfish, caring love, a love that was concerned for the well-being of the other person. Some commentators do not attach any connection to Jesus' statement in John 13:34, but I am convinced that there is a connection from the fact that John wrote both statements and also from the fact that this is the only sense in which I can understand the "new" and the "old" commandment about loving one's brother.

2:8 Yet I am writing you a new command; its truth is seen in him and you,

The Law of Moses had taught that one should love one's neighbor as oneself. Jesus' love went even farther than this. Jesus told them to love "even as I have loved you" (John 13:34). This "new" love, *agapē*, was not necessarily a love that responded to others' love (this was implied by *philos*, a brotherly love or a reciprocal love).

because the darkness is passing and the true light is already shining.

Here in verse 8, John applies all of this to those false teachers. He is identifying love, the new love, as the **true light . . . already shining.** If Jesus is the light, and John has already argued that he is, then to love as Jesus loved would be to shine in the lives of others with the light of Jesus' love. Therefore, if one did not love, the darkness was taking over. The darkness (a strong element of the Gnostics' teaching) is passing away among those who love as Jesus loved. Obeying the commands of Jesus will assure us that we are "in the light" (see v. 7).

56

F. IN THE LIGHT OR IN THE DARKNESS (2:9-11)

⁹Anyone who claims to be in the light but hates his brother is still in the darkness. ¹⁰Whoever loves his brother lives in the light, and there is nothing in him to make him stumble. ¹¹But whoever hates his brother is in the darkness and walks around in the darkness; he does not know where he is going, because the darkness has blinded him.

ᵃ10 Or it

The Gnostics saw darkness as being related to the evil god, or the god who created matter. Darkness, therefore, was to be avoided, they believed. They believed that the "light" represented by the good god, whom incidentally they regarded as the father of Jesus Christ, was to be looked for. In these two verses, John is facing the real meaning of light: it involves loving one's brother. He is not confining love to this, for if one has love for the Father, he will also love his brother (see 4:20).

The expression "the love of God" has at least three possible meanings. It can refer to the love that God has for man; or man's love for God; or, God's kind of love. These three points of view are discussed in some detail by Marshall.[8] It is not likely that John made such a line of distinction as this, but he probably saw all of these three meanings intertwining throughout the whole concept of love. Notice in the previous paragraph (see v. 5) that if anyone obeys the word of God, "God's love is truly made complete in him." Love that is complete is love that has matured or reached its ultimate goal. "Made complete" is a translation of τετελείωται (*teteleiōtai*, "has been perfected"). This is a perfect tense, passive voice of its verb form. It signifies that it has been perfected (completed action) from a force outside of itself. The word suggests that the perfection has come from no act of its own. Obviously, the one who has been acting is Jesus Christ. We

---

[8]Marshall, *The Epistles of John*, p. 124ff.

need to remember that love, or any other characteristic of humanity, is never completely perfect until it has been "made perfect" by the cross of Jesus.

Love is the very essence of God. Later on in this epistle (4:16) we are told that "God is love." God's love surely showed an unselfish concern for all the world in that he gave his only Son for our salvation. We must recognize that if God's love is ever demonstrated in our lives, we will need to demonstrate an unselfish concern for God and his will. In our everyday language, we think and speak of "perfection" or "perfect" as that without error or flaw. The Greek word for perfect is τέλειος (teleios, "complete, mature, perfect") and we must make God's love perfect in us by walking as Jesus walked (see vv. 5,6).

2:9 Anyone who claims to be in the light but hates his brother is still in the darkness.

Living in the light has no place for hatred. Love can abide only in a life lived in the light. If we claim that we love our brother, but we are living in the darkness — that is, out of fellowship with Christ who is the Light — we lie and do not have the truth. John's concept of love is different from what ours often is. Marshall makes this distinction: "We would say that there are persons whom we do not love, but this is not the same thing as hating them. . . . Our attitude is a neutral one. . . . But John will have none of this. His concept of love is caring for the needs of others, even to the point of self-sacrifice. If I am unwilling to to do that for somebody in need, I love myself more than him. . . ."[9]

2:10 Whoever loves his brother lives in the light, and there is nothing in him to make him stumble.

Here is another of John's stylistic device of stating a fact and then giving the opposite. In verse 9, John expresses the

---

[9]Ibid., p. 131.

negative idea of hating a brother and remaining in darkness;
here, whoever loves his brother is in the light. Failing to live
in the light places one in the darkness and here people stumble. What a beautiful analogy: how many of us have tried to
walk in the darkness of night and have stumbled? The one
who "lives in the light" has no reason to stumble for the light
shows him the way. The same is true of the Christian. If we
walk in the light, we can see by the direction from Jesus how
to walk without stumbling.

**2:11 But whoever hates his brother is in the darkness and
walks around in the darkness; he does not know where he is
going, because the darkness has blinded him.**
Again, John uses the opposite to emphasize the role of
"Light" and "Darkness." John uses four verbs here in this passage: "*hates* his brother," "*walks* around in darkness," "*does
not know* where he is going," and "darkness *has blinded* him."
The first three are in the active voice, indicating that the subject is doing the acting." The fourth verb is in the passive
voice, indicating that the subject is acted upon. This is significant in our understanding of how we behave. Lenski discusses
the individual who walks in darkness as "one of the haters
who has turned heretic and hates the brethren that are true
to the Word and refuse to give it up at his bending. He is
bent on being a *skandalon,* on dragging others into the night
of spiritual death, into the same night in which he is, in which
he walks, which has made his own eyes blind."[10] The word
σκάνδαλον (*skandalon,* "a snare, a stumbling-block") is used in
verse 10 of one who would make others stumble. John is definitely referring to those who have left the body of believers
and have become gnostic heretics.
To "hate a brother," "walk in darkness," and "fail to know"
are all the fault of the person. We must *actively* conduct our

---

[10]R.C.H. Lenski, *The Interpretation of the Epistles of St. Peter, St. John, and
St. Jude* (Minneapolis: Augsburg, 1966), p. 416.

lives so that we are living in Christ. One who is walking in the
dark is the same as a blind person. This was a strong statement
to be making to those false teachers who did not have the proper understanding and appreciation of Jesus, but who thought
they were the bearers of light! John is not suggesting in these
verses that the Christians he is addressing are blind or not obedient. He is referring to those who are stirring up the hearts
and minds of those Christians. He is referring to the Gnostics!

G. JOHN'S REASONS FOR WRITING (2:12-14)

I write to you, dear children,
  because your sins have been forgiven on account of his
  name.
I write to you, fathers,
  because you have known him who is from beginning.
I write to you, young men,
  because you have overcome the evil one.
I write to you, dear children,
  because you have known the Father.
I write to you, fathers,
  because you have known him who is from the beginning.
I write to you, young men,
  because you are strong,
  and the word of God lives in you,
  and you have overcome the evil one.

This is a rather unusual section of 1 John. John addresses
several groups of people on why he has written to them. "I
write to you" occurs six times here and five times throughout
the rest of the book: 1:4 (with "we"); 2:1,8,26; and 5:13. He
uses the same expression in a negative form at least twice.
Whether he is attempting to establish his credibility by using
this expression or whether there is another reason for this

sentence construction, there is wide opinion. Another strange
sentence structure is the use of the present tense for "I write"
in the first statement (vv. 12-13) and the aorist for "I wrote" in
the second sentence (v. 14).

In these six references to "dear children," "fathers,"
"young men," and by implication the opposite sex must be
included, John is using endearing words to show his love for
them. All of these terms are endearing terms. John evidently
wants his readers to know the reason for his writing, for he
mentions it more than a dozen times in the epistle. It was
important for those Christians to realize the solemnity and
seriousness of the heretical movement beginning among
them. It is interesting to note that John addresses three
groups of people, as noted above, and he addresses each of
them twice. "Dear children" are admonished in verses 12 and
13; all three groups are addressed in verse 13; and "fathers"
and "young men" are addressed in verse 14. Why he has
selected these three groups we do not know. Stott suggests
that Augustine and other Latin commentators favored "the
view . . . that they represent three different stages of spiritual
pilgrimage: the *little children* are those newborn in Christ; the
young men are more developed Christians, strong and victorious in spiritual warfare; while the *fathers* possess the depth
and stability of ripe Christian experience" (italics added).[11]

**2:12 I write to you, dear children,[12] because your sins have
been forgiven on account of his name.**

In the first of these six statements, John says **your sins
have been forgiven on account of his name.** John strikes
another strong blow at his opponents. In the first place, he
asserts that they have sins, or else how could they be forgiven

---

[11]Stott, *The Letters of John,* p. 101.
[12]The word here is τεκνία (*teknia*) which means "little children." He is
probably using the word here to indicate not "little children," signifying
young of age, but in terms of their spiritual age. But, of this, we cannot be
sure. It just seems more appropriate in terms of the context.

of them (see vv. 8-10)? In the second place, this was accomplished on account of "his name." This strikes at the gnostic belief that Jesus only seemed to be human, for it is implied that Jesus' sacrifice had something to do with the forgiveness.

2:13 I write to you, fathers, because you have known him who is from the beginning.

Because they are identical statements, we are discussing verse 13a and 14a together. Why John has both of these identical statements is not known. See the comment at the end of the section of Scripture. Above we noted that the chronological age of the "little children" was not intended. If chronological age is intended, then we are at a loss to know why he uses *teknia* in one reference and *paidia* in the other one. By the same logic, the expression "fathers" referred not to chronological age, but to experience in knowing the Lord, or spiritual maturity. They have known him from the beginning. It seems safe to assume that these "fathers" he is addressing may have actually known Jesus, or at least they were personally aware of him in some way. These fathers were probably the "spiritual" fathers rather than physical fathers. Stott suggests that they may "have progressed into a deep communion with God."[13] A continuity of the message of Jesus must be very important, for in both of these references to the "fathers," he gives the same admonition, **because you have known him who is from the beginning** (verses 13b and 14).

I write to you, young men,[14] because you have overcome the evil one.

Again, John opposes the Gnostics' concept that Christians do not sin (see comments on 1:8–2:2). There may be an

---

[13]Stott, *The Letters of John*, p. 102.

[14]"Young men," νεανίσκοι, the nominative plural of νεανίσκος (*neaniskos*, "a young man, a youth"). It is a word which has also been translated by the term "soldier." This gives us an idea of the approximate age of those John was addressing.

implied compliment that John is giving the "young men" who have had the ability to "overcome the evil one." The language here is such that John recognizes that these "young men" have conquered, or overcome, the evil one.

I write to you, dear children, because you have known the Father.

This third part of verse 3 is the second statement to the "dear children." There are at least two differences from the previous statement in verse 12. First of all, a different word is used in the Greek to reference the children. It is παιδία (*paidia*), plural of the noun παιδίον (*paidion*, (little child"). This is a diminutive form of expression and does refer to "infants" or "little children." Is John referring to the same "little children" of verse 12? It should be noted that this time there is a different "because" statement. The first statement was written "because your sins have been forgiven." This present statement was written **because you have known the Father.** In a sense, they are saying the same thing because when one comes to the Father, his sins are forgiven. Obedience to the commands (or commandments) of God will bring about forgiveness.

2:14 I write to you, fathers, because you have known him who is from the beginning. I write to you, young men, because you are strong, and the word of God lives in you, and you have overcome the evil one.

As we noted above, the first line is an identical repetition of verse 13a. Some commentators agree that the "young men" were a group of Christians who were younger, less mature than the "fathers," yet they were dedicated, energetic Christians who nevertheless would be susceptible to false teaching. Hence, John felt the need to warn them of the dangers they faced. They were Christians in whom the Word of God dwells which has helped them to withstand the "evil one." Perhaps John is commending these "young men" for their strength and ability to withstand evil teaching.

Some commentators suggest that John is using the "little children" expression to refer to all of the Christians and that there are, in reality, only two groups he is referring to: the "young men" and "fathers."[15] There appears to be no definitive answer to this triple pattern of groups in the church, nor a compelling explanation of why they are given twice. There is a wide range of opinions on the nature and purpose of the six statements.

H. CHRISTIANS AND THE WORLD (2:15-17)

[15]Do not love the world or anything in the world. If anyone loves the world, the love of the Father is not in him. [16]For everything in the world — the cravings of sinful man, the lust of his eyes and the boasting of what he has and does — comes not from the Father but from the world. [17]The world and its desires pass away, but the man who does the will of God lives forever.

The word "world" (κόσμος, kosmos) is used at least 20 times in this epistle: 2:2,15,16,17; 3:1; 4:1,3,4,5,9,14,17; 5:4,5,19. It is used to mean different things. Marshall notes that "It ['world'] can refer in quite a neutral way to the created universe which God made to be 'very good' (Gen. 1:31). But in the writings of John 'world' signifies more usually mankind organized in rebellion against God, so that the word carries a negative sense. It is under the control of the evil one. . . ."[16]

2:15 Do not love the world or anything in the world.
Much of the world in which John lived saw the world in terms of a conflict of forces. The Gnostics, for example, saw the world from the point of view of two gods: the god of the Old Testament, the creator of good and evil, the Demiurge;

---

[15]Refer to I. Howard Marshall, *The Epistles of John*, pp. 137-138.
[16]Marshall, *The Epistles of John*, p. 142.

and the god of the New Testament, a loving, caring God, the father of Jesus Christ. The world was often viewed as an enemy to good and right. Peter, in his first epistle, reminded his audience that we are "strangers in the world" (1 Pet 1:1). He also wrote "I urge you, as aliens and strangers in the world, to abstain from sinful desires, which war against your soul" (1 Pet 2:11). Paul also reminds us that we are not a part of the world (Eph 2:11-12). So, it is not strange that John would warn his readers **do not love the world**.

This admonition should not be interpreted as saying that we should hate the physical world, for it is God's creation. This admonition by John is not recommending that Christians should separate themselves totally from the world. Jesus told his Father that he did not want the disciples to leave the world, "but that you protect them from the evil one. They are not of the world, even as I am not of it" (John 17:15-16). We are not to become attached to the world in the sense that we do not want to join Jesus in the place he is preparing for us (see John 14:1ff.). This world is not our final home, but it is only the place where we prepare for the home in heaven.

If anyone loves the world, the love of the Father is not in him.
Again, John is not urging that we hate this world. We must learn to "be content whatever the circumstances" and learn "the secret of being content in any and every situation" (Phil 4:11-12). What John is recommending is that we not participate in the worldly things and become tied to the world. For, if we do this, the Father is not in us.

2:16 For everything in the world — the cravings of sinful man, the lust of his eyes and the boasting of what he has and does — comes not from the Father but from the world.
Here, John more specifically defines what he means by loving the world. There are three types of temptation that he delineates: "lust of the flesh," or "the cravings of sinful man,"

"the lust of his eyes," and "the pride of life," or "the boasting of what he has and does." Humankind has always been much the same. The temptations of our present day, or of John's day, are not much different from those temptations in the Garden of Eden. God had told them not to touch the Tree of the Knowledge of Good and Evil. But, when Satan tempted Eve, and ultimately Adam, Scripture says "When the woman saw that the fruit of the tree was good for food [lust of the flesh], and pleasing to the eye [lust of the eye], and also desirable for gaining wisdom [pride of life], she took some and ate it. She also gave some to her husband who was with her, and he ate it" (Gen 3:6). We are not saying that because something is good to eat or beautiful to look at or will cause us pleasure, that it is always wrong, but in *this* case it is true because God had specifically commanded that they *not* eat of it.

Again, look at the temptation of Jesus. Satan presented three temptations to Jesus. He appealed to his fleshly desires. Jesus was fasting, but Satan told him to turn stones into bread. Satan took Jesus "to the holy city and had him stand on the highest point of the temple" and tempted him to "throw [himself] down" and God would save him. Jesus responded with, "Do not put the Lord your God to the test." And, third, Satan "took him to a very high mountain and showed him all the kingdoms of the world and their splendor." Implied is the idea, "Look how all these people will see you and revere you." Satan said, "If you will bow down and worship me, I will give you all these kingdoms," but Jesus ordered Satan to go away; he would worship only God (see Matthew 4:1-10). Isn't it interesting that in the Garden of Eden and at the wilderness of Jesus' temptation, sin presented itself in three types of temptation, and now John warns against the same ones? He warned his readers of lust of the flesh, lust of the eye, and pride of life.

2:17 The world and its desires pass away, but the man who does the will of God lives forever. There is good reason for us to avoid the world and all of its allurements: the new age, the Christian age, has come. All that does not come from the will of God will eventually be doomed. John clearly says, **the world and its desires pass away.**[17] Only one group of people will remain: those who do the will of God. They will live forever. Those who were refusing to accept the full message of God should have felt the strength of John's argument. For that day, as well as for our own day, humanity must obey the commands of God's choice, not its own. In our age of wanting to make our own decisions, we must carefully follow what God wants rather than what we want.

I. WARNINGS AGAINST ANTICHRISTS (2:18-27)

[18]**Dear children, this is the last hour; and as you have heard that the antichrist is coming, even now many antichrists have come. This is how we now it is the last hour.** [19]**They went out from us, but they did not really belong to us. For if they had belonged to us, they would have remained with us; but their going showed that none of them belonged to us.**
[20]**But you have an anointing from the Holy One, and all of you know the truth.**[a] [21]**I do not write to you because you do not know the truth, but because you do know it and because no lie comes from the truth.** [22]**Who is the liar? It is the man who denies that Jesus is the Christ. Such a man is the antichrist — he denies the Father and the Son.** [23]**No one who denies the Son has the Father; whoever acknowledges the Son has the Father also.**

---

[17]The word for "is passing away" is παράγεται (*paragetai*). This word has the force of saying "is already disintegrating," according to Stott, *The Letters of John*, pp. 105-106.

²⁴See that what you have heard from the beginning remains in you. If it does, you also will remain in the Son and in the Father. ²⁵And this is what he promised us — even eternal life.

²⁶I am writing these things to you about those who are trying to lead you astray. ²⁷As for you, the anointing you received from him remains in you, and you do not need anyone to teach you. But as his anointing teaches you about all things and as that anointing is real, not counterfeit — just as it has taught you, remain in him.

ª20 Some manuscripts *and you know all things*

2:18 Dear children,

John has alluded to the false teachers earlier in this epistle, but this is the most biting reference to them yet. There is an urgency to this message. John begins this discussion with his loving statement "my little children" (*paidia*). It is obvious that this is a term of endearment, for he has already addressed the "young men" and "fathers." The message here appears to be specially important to John by the use of this diminutive form of παῖς (*pais*, child).[18]

this is the last hour;

Some commentators hold that John is teaching that the "old age" is about to pass away and that Jesus will be returning shortly. It is true that John states that it is the "last hour" or the last age. Several references are made to the "last times" in various places in the New Testament. Peter declared, referring to the astounding presence of the Holy Spirit on Pentecost, that "this is what was spoken by the prophet Joel: '*In the last days* [emphasis mine] God says, I will pour out my Spirit on

---

[18]The reader may wish to consult a fuller discussion of the use of "my little child" in John's writing and compare it to other words he uses. See Bruce, *The Epistles of John*, p. 48.

COLLEGE PRESS NIV COMMENTARY

all people'" (Acts 2:16-17). Paul uses the same kind of language in 1 Timothy 4:1, "The Spirit clearly says that **in later times** some will abandon the faith." (See also Isa 2:2; Dan 12:9; Micah 4:1; 2 Tim 2:17; and 2 Pet 3:3.) All of these references are to the fact that Jesus brought a new age, as opposed to the age marked by the Law of Moses. This is indeed the last time, and at the end of these days, Jesus will return, but we know neither the day nor the hour when he will come; neither did John.

and as you have heard that the antichrist is coming, even now many antichrists have come. This is how we know it is the last hour.
The term "antichrist" is not found in early Christian times outside of Christian circles. Although the concept of an antichrist was spoken of in other writings, the word ἀντιχρίστος (*antichristos*, "antichrist," i.e. one standing in opposition or competition to Christ) is found only in John's epistles in 1 John 2:18,22; 4:3; 2 John 7. There were many early Christians who were looking for the "antichrist." Such enemies of Christ had been predicted, though not using this word, by Paul and others. The presence of these "antichrists" of John's day was regarded as proof of their existence; hence, he writes **This is how we know it is the last hour,** namely, by their appearance. It must be the last days. The absence of the definite article before "last hour" in the Greek text is assumed by some commentators to mean that the presence of these false teachers is "last hour kind of behavior." Perhaps John is saying that this is "a signal or sign of the last hour."[19] Earlier, it was stated that this was not necessarily a declaration of the time of the Second Coming or *parousia* (παρουσία, "coming or second coming of Jesus"). As we noted earlier, Jesus said no one knows the day or hour of his coming, not even he himself. It is true, however,

---

[19]Roberts, *The Letters of John*, p. 62.

that many "antichrists," or adversaries of the Christ, were appearing by the end of the first century when this epistle was written. John, this apostle of love but who was described by Christ earlier as a "son of thunder," is speaking very harshly of these enemies of Jesus who are declaring that his earthly existence was only a figment of their imagination or only seemed to take place. Jesus had warned that "false Christs and false prophets will appear and perform great signs and miracles to deceive the elect — if that were possible. See, I have told you ahead of time" (Matthew 24:24-25).

2:19 They went out from us, but they did not really belong to us. For if they had belonged to us, they would have remained with us; but their going showed that none of them belonged to us.

Although John has not yet specifically identified who these false teachers are, he does indicate that they had been with them. It would appear that these who **went out from us** had at one time been Christians, but they may have not been deeply converted. At what point these individuals turned their backs on the church, we do not know. The gnostic movement certainly began during or before the first century. The apostle Paul warns of departures from the truth: "The Spirit clearly says that in later times some will abandon the faith and follow deceiving spirits and things taught by demons. Such teachings come through hypocritical liars, whose consciences have been seared as with a hot iron" (1 Tim 4:1). He then delineates some of the false teachings they promoted, some of which were clearly practiced by some of the Gnostics of the first and second centuries.

John seems willing to separate these faithful Christians from those who went away. He says that their going away **showed that none of them belong to us.** There comes a time when false teaching begins to be promoted that church leaders, specifically the elders, need to "mark" those heresy promoters and not allow them to bring division in the body.

2:20 But you have an anointing from the Holy One, and all of you know the truth.

John turns his attention away from "those who went away" to those who are still among the faithful. Those faithful "children" have been protected from the evil one. They **have an anointing from the Holy One.** The word "anointing" is the word χρίσμα (*chrisma*). It is highly possible that John is making a play on words. "Christ" is a translation of χριστός (*christos*, "Christ," or "the anointed one"). The first four letters (or, in English, the first five) are the same in both words. But, at any rate, we have an anointing from Christ, or the Holy Spirit. Whichever he means here, it is a divine anointing from the Godhead.

2:21 I do not write to you because you do not know the truth, but because you do know it and because no lie comes from the truth.

The anointing has made the true believers to know the truth. The anointing comes from the truth. Therefore, those who have remained faithful to the "anointing" have the truth and are not liars. I recommend that the reader look at John 14, 15, and 16, where Jesus tells the apostles that he will send to them the Holy Spirit. The anointing of the apostles with the Holy Spirit cannot be ignored, for it is in their receiving of the Holy Spirit that God and his Son should be revealed to us.

2:22 Who is the liar? It is the man who denies that Jesus is the Christ. Such a man is the antichrist — he denies the Father and the Son.

Who is the liar? John asks. The Gnostics believed that they had a secret revelation or knowledge from God. It was a special knowledge for their own group which made them some sort of a special class of individuals — a "notch above" normal Christians. John answers his own question by saying the liar **is the man who denies that Jesus is the Christ.** This is a description of the docetic Gnostic. There is no room for fellowship between God and heretics. By their own acceptance of "the lie," they have severed their fellowship with God. Satan is the liar; the Gnostic who is a follower of Satan is the liar. This is the force of John's charge. **Such a man is the antichrist — he denies the Father and the Son.** This is the first time that John actually identifies who is the antichrist, the adversary, of Christ. He is the one who denies the humanity of Jesus. This charge is levelled directly at the docetic element of Gnosticism.

We cannot be certain of all that the Gnostics taught. It is almost universally accepted that the Gnostics of John's day were greatly influenced by the teachings of Cerinthus. However, it is likely that they did not accept all of Cerinthus's teachings. Cerinthus believed and taught the Adoption concept of Jesus' Sonship. In other words, Cerinthus believed that at some time, probably at his baptism, he was adopted by God, as we indicated earlier. We do not have any indication in John's epistle that the Gnostics of his time accepted this.[20]

2:23 No one who denies the Son has the Father; whoever acknowledges the Son has the Father also.

The real gravity of the gnostic theology is seen in this verse. Not only does the docetic teaching that Jesus was not a physical reality, that is, Jesus *only seemed* to be human, make the believer in Docetism a liar, but it also makes him deny *both* the Father and the Son. Confession of the Son seems to be a requirement of possessing or "having" the Father. In other words, "you can't have one without the other." These heretics could not have the Father without accepting Jesus as his Son.

---

[20]Marshall states, "The difficulty is that we do not know what they taught positively; John is content to tell us what they denied. Did they give their allegiance to Jesus as a mere man? Or did they, on the other hand, believe in the Messiah/Son of God but deny that he had become incarnate and died for human sin? On the whole, it seems most probable that they accepted Jesus in some sense, but denied that he was the Messiah and Son of God . . ." Marshall, *The Epistles of John*, p. 158.

2:24 See that what you have heard from the beginning remains in you. If it does, you also will remain in the Son and in the Father.

In such a time of spiritual frustration, it is important for these first century Christians to have an anchor. John urges them to remain in the things which they have heard from the beginning: the pure gospel of Jesus Christ. Again, as in previous places, **the beginning** refers to the beginning of the Christian age, or at least their initial confrontation with the gospel. We, in the modern world, ought to be faithful to what was taught in the beginning rather than chase after new fads and innovations of religious practice. John is urging his readers to cling to the original Christian message. He promises that if they do, they will **remain in the Son and in the Father.**

2:25 And this is what he promised us — even eternal life.

There is a reward for those who remain faithful, John promises. It is not so evident in this reference as it is later in the epistle, but this **eternal life** is not a "there and then" situation, but it is a "here and now" promise. John is very clear on the fact that our eternal life begins in *this life,* and we do not have to wait until later for it to begin. See 1 John 5:12 as an example of what John was revealing. Eternal life is in the present tense. On the other hand, John is not saying that there is an eternal security once one has been born again: it is possible for us to lose the eternal life by not remaining in Jesus.

2:26 I am writing these things to you about those who are trying to lead you astray.

Here is another of the "I am writing. . ." statements. We have noted that this expression occurs at least eleven times in the epistle. This time, the purpose that he is writing to them about is **those who are trying to lead you astray.** This short statement gives us an important glance into the activities of the heretics: they were evangelistic in their efforts. Not only were they holding these views themselves, but they were

73

evidently active in their proselyting activities. They were seeking to evangelize recruits from the believers. John is writing about this; he is warning them of their tactics. Their aim was "to lead you astray."

2:27 As for you, the anointing you received from him remains in you, and you do not need anyone to teach you. But as his anointing teaches you about all things and as that anointing is real, not counterfeit — just as it has taught you, remain in him.

John wants them to know that he is not overly concerned about them, just being cautious. First, he has warned them about gnostic heresy (v. 26); second, they (at least, some of them) have known the Lord from the beginning; third, they have received an anointing from Jesus and from the Father.

III. GOD'S LOVE FOR US/OUR LOVE FOR ONE ANOTHER (2:28-3:24)

A. CHILDREN OF GOD (2:28-29)

[28]**And now, dear children, continue in him, so that when he appears we may be confident and unashamed before him at his coming.**
[29]**If you know that he is righteous, you know that everyone who does what is right has been born of him.**

At this point, John makes a transition from the polemic approach to a more exhortative and practical approach. He temporarily ends the warnings of the Gnostics and their false teaching and begins a more loving, relational message. What is our relationship to God? How does the fact that we are children of God affect our everyday living? How will the recognition that we are the children of God affect our relationship with each other and with the concept of right and wrong? It is important for us to realize that God is a loving, caring God rather than a despotic, and punitive God. So, these two verses and the first section of the third chapter are an explanation of who we are and how we relate to God.

2:28 And now, dear children, continue in him,
The term, **And now**, is undoubtedly used to indicate that he is beginning a new topic. John opens this new topic by talking about the importance of continuity in Christ Jesus. The NIV translates this **continue in him . . . .** Others have translated it "And now, dear children, abide in him. . . ." The Greek for the last three words is μένετε ἐν αὐτῷ (*menete en autō*, "abide in him"). The NIV translators were probably wanting to show not only a one-time abiding, but a continuous abiding. The use of the word "abide" seems to me to be a stronger relationship to Jesus or the Father. And the use of the present, active, indicative verb form actually shows a continuous abiding, not a one-time abiding. Earlier, John has shown that those who "know God," who "have God," and those in whom God abides are those in whom God's word abides. Furthermore, he has told us that "this is what he promised us — even eternal life" (2:25).

so that when he appears we may be confident and unashamed before him at his coming.
John reminds his readers of the return[21] of Jesus. We must be prepared with the indwelling of Jesus, or his abiding in us. We do not want to "shrink from shame at his coming." If Jesus is abiding in us, or if we continue in him, we will have

---

[21]Παρουσία (*parousia*, "presence, coming, advent") is generally used to refer to the *second* coming of Jesus. This is certainly what is meant by this reference. But the word used here is not παρουσία, but φανερωθῇ, (*phanerōthē*, "he might be shown, made known, revealed"). This word has more of a revealing, or making public in a more open way which is the intention of Scripture. Christ will appear and "every eye will see him" (Rev 1:7).

no reason to be ashamed at his coming. We will be in a continuing fellowship with him. "Confidence" is often translated as "boldness" in some translations.[22] In this context, John's statement later on in the epistle, "there is no fear in love," takes on a special meaning (see 4:18). John wants us to be prepared so that we will be **unashamed**,[23] or that we will not be made to be ashamed when he comes. We should strive to live in such a manner that we can stand before him with boldness. In Jesus' first coming, he came to be our Savior and he died on the cross to bring that about. In his second coming, he will be our judge, and we need to be prepared for that. Earlier, we discussed the φανερωθῇ (phanerōthē) of Jesus as compared with the παρουσία (parousia). Actually these two words complement each other. The manifestation of Jesus (phanerōthē) will take place when he comes again. This is the time when John hopes that his readers will not be made ashamed because they will have walked as Jesus walked.

2:29 If you know that he is righteous, you know that everyone who does what is right has been born of him.

John introduces a new thought not discussed before. That is that we have **been born of him**. He appears to be changing the "person" in this verse. Nowhere in the New Testament are we told to be "born of Christ." Even Jesus (see John 3:1ff.) did not represent himself as being the source of the new birth. Throughout the New Testament, "born of" refers to God.

---

[22]From παρρησίαν (parrēsian, "courage, confidence, boldness, fearlessness, esp. in the presence of persons of high rank.") This is a strong word, indicating that there is fearlessness. See William F. Arndt and F. Wilbur Gingrich, *A Greek-English Lexicon of the New Testament and Other Early Christian Literature* (Chicago and London: The University of Chicago Press, 1979), pp. 630-631.

[23]The word for "unashamed" is μὴ αἰσχυνθῶμεν (mē aischynthōmen, "not be made shamed"). This is a passive form of the verb. The NIV translates this "that we may be unashamed." "That we may not be ashamed before him when he comes" may be a little more accurate.

John states that **if you know that he is righteous** then you will know that those who do right have "been born of him." He represents "righteousness," not "knowledge" as that which makes us *know* they have been born again. Is this a subtle jab at the Gnostics? They would have claimed that their "special" knowledge would be the source of being born again, not righteousness. This introduction of the regeneration or being born of him is a very natural transition into the next chapter and our being children of God.

1 JOHN 3

B. GOD'S LOVE FOR HIS CHILDREN (3:1-3)

[1]How great is the love the Father has lavished on us, that we should be called children of God! And that is what we are! The reason the world does not know us is that it did not know him. [2]Dear friends, now we are children of God, and what we will be has not yet been made known. But we know that when he appears[a], we shall be like him, for we shall see him as he is. [3]Everyone who has this hope in him purifies himself, just as he is pure"

[a]2 Or *when it is made known*

3:1 How great is the love the Father has lavished on us,

The word translated "lavished" is from δίδωμι (*didōmi*, "to give"). However when we think of the awesomeness of having God give to us, it does become lavish. God has granted to us physical being, everyday blessings, health, the ability to be happy, and on top of all of this, a spiritual fellowship with him and his Son Jesus Christ. When God, "who owns all the cattle on a thousand hills" (Ps 50:10) gives to us, then we should be deeply humbled! We sustain a very special relation with God. The world does not have that kind of a relationship. And the world does not realize how greatly blessed we are because "it did not know him." There is a cause-relation kinship between the world knowing us and the world knowing God. They did not know God, so they could not know us. The greatest wonder of all is that we are children of God!

None of us has had anything to do with who our natural parents are. But in the case of our Heavenly Father, we make a determined choice. God does not force us to become his children. We obey his commands, and he makes us his children. There is a parallel between this verse and Jesus' teaching to Nicodemus about the new birth (John 3:1-3). It is not because of our own righteousness that we are children of God. It is brought about because of God's great love for us.

that we should be called children of God! And that is what we are! The reason the world does not know us is that it did not know him.

John makes a strong exclamation: we are to **be called children of God.** And then to emphasize his thought he adds, **And that is what we are!** Again, he stresses that the world does not know us. The reason? Because **it did not know him.** These Gnostics, the false teachers, do not know us because they do not know God! Earlier, John stated that they are not of us. "If they had belonged to us, they would have remained with us" (see 1 John 2:19).

3:2 Dear friends,[1] now we are children of God,

Some emphasis seems to be given to the word "now." We know what we are **now: we are children of God.** John makes three statements which represent the sequence of some events to follow: first, when he shall appear (v. 1); second, we shall be like him, (v. 2); and , third, we shall see him as he is. Of this we can be assured. All of this is because we are children of God. No one has ever seen God (John 6:46). The nearest anyone has come was to see Jesus, for he said "Anyone who has seen me has seen the Father" (John 14:9).

---

[1]This is a much stronger statement in the Greek: ἀγαπητοί (*agapētoi*, "dear, beloved, indicating a strong relationship," see Arndt & Gingrich, *Greek-English Lexicon*, p. 6). It is much more than "dear friends"; it is "dearly beloved."

We know what we are now; we are children of the Father in heaven. We know some things about our earthly existence as part of the fellowship of God. We know that angels and the prophets longed to see and experience what we enjoy. "Concerning this salvation, the prophets, who spoke of the grace that was to come to you, searched intently and with the greatest care, trying to find out the time and circumstances to which the Spirit of Christ in them was pointing when he predicted the sufferings of Christ and the glories that would follow. It was revealed to them that they were not serving themselves but you, when they spoke of the things that have now been told you by those who have preached the gospel to you by the Holy Spirit sent from heaven. Even angels long to look into these things" (1 Pet 1:10-12).

and what we will be has not yet been made known. But we know that when he appears, we shall be like him, for we shall see him as he is.
     One of the reasons that we cannot know what he is now is because we do not have the ability to peer into the spiritual realm. Our language and our understanding is not sufficient to look into the spiritual and eternal realm. This is one reason why **what we will be has not yet been made known.** God has not revealed to us the manner of transformation we will experience when we meet our Savior. But we are assured that we will experience a transformation. Paul told the Corinthian Christians that "we, who with unveiled faces all reflect the Lord's glory, are being transformed into his likeness with ever-increasing glory, which comes from the Lord, who is the Spirit" (2 Cor 3:18). The Gnostics would not have understood what John is saying. How can one who was human (as Jesus was) also be a spiritual, eternal being; and how can he at his coming make us to be like he is? Undoubtedly, John is establishing a very important concept for those who did not follow the heretics who had left them. Why would they want to follow them when the privileges of following Christ were so magnificent and awe-inspiring? What

81

John is saying is that "this transformation will take place because we shall see him as he is."[2]

3:3 Everyone who has this hope in him purifies himself, just as he is pure.

This hope is obviously referring to the hope that we will be changed and will be like him. It is a hope that is in him (that is, in Jesus).[3] It is not surprising that John would connect our being like him to the concept of purity. Jesus was pure and he stressed purity. This would be in contradistinction to the Gnostics' denial of sin (see 1:8–2:2) and to the impurity of the lives of some of the Gnostics we read about in ancient literature. Some of them taught and practiced "free love," and if there is no sin, they undoubtedly practiced other activities that would tend to be impure.

Purity does not come to the Christian through anything the Christian *is* or *has done*. Purity comes about through the shedding of Jesus' blood on the cross. The docetic Gnostics denied that Jesus died on the cross. He only *seemed* to die. John has emphasized before that since Christ is righteous, we need to practice righteousness (through obedience to his commands) if we expect to be righteous. Nothing but the blood of Christ can remove the guilt and stain of sin on our lives (see 1:7; 1 Pet 1:22; 2 Cor 7:1).

C. WARNINGS AGAINST SIN (3:4-10)

[4]**Everyone who sins breaks the law; in fact, sin is lawlessness. [5]But you know that he appeared so that he might take away our sins. And in him is no sin. [6]No one who lives in**

---

[2]Marshall, *The Epistles of John*, pp. 172-173.

[3]Some translators use "in him" and others use "on him" for ἐπ' αὐτῷ (*ep' autō*, "in" or "on" him). The "him" referred to here must be Jesus. This is further substantiated by the use of the reflexive ἑαυτόν, (*heauton*, "himself"). The translation would be "as he himself" is pure.

him keeps on sinning. No one who continues to sin has
either seen him or known him.
⁷Dear children, do not let anyone lead you astray. He
who does what is right is righteous, just as he is righteous.
⁸He who does what is sinful is of the devil, because the devil
has been sinning from the beginning. The reason the Son of
God appeared was to destroy the devil's work. ⁹No one who
is born of God will continue to sin, because God's seed
remains in him; he cannot go on sinning, because he has
been born of God. ¹⁰This is how we know who the children
of God are and who the children of the devil are: Anyone
who does not do what is right is not a child of God; nor is
anyone who does not love his brother.

Again, John makes a sudden change in the thought. It is all
connected to his central theme, which is to discredit those
"who went out from them." The gnostic philosophy did not
have any place in it for a doctrine of sin. If one had the "special" gift of knowledge that they claimed to have, he was above
sin. In the first part of this section of Scripture, John begins
first by telling us about the nature of sin and the sinner.

3:4 Everyone who sins breaks the law; in fact, sin is lawlessness.
Paul pointed out this same truth to the Romans. It was
through the law that Paul learned about sin. The law itself is
not sin, but disobeying what the law said was sin (see Rom
7:7-12). It does not appear here that the "law" is referring to
the Law of Moses. Rather, sin appears to be just the opposite
of righteousness. Righteousness has already been described as
obedience of the commands, or commandments, given to us
through the Son. So, as Jesus is righteous, so we also should be
righteous when we obey the commands. This in no way is giving us the ability to be righteous on our own. It is through the
shedding of Jesus' blood that we are made righteous. Living a
lawless life is living as if there were no law. There were two

Commission *Omission* major approaches to the definition of sin in John's day. Lawlessness (ἀνομίαν, *anomian*, "no law") was one form. To the Jewish population, this would be very clear, for they were bound by the law. The other meaning of sin was the Greek concept of sin, "missing the mark," from the Greek word ἁμαρτία (*hamartia*, literally, "missing the mark" or "sin"). John uses the word *hamartia* here when he says "sin is lawlessness." He covers both of these meanings here in his text.

3:5 But you know that he appeared so that he might take away our sins. And in him is no sin.

This was the redeeming work of Jesus. The verb used here is not the one used for "to atone for" but rather "to take away, to bear away." Jesus was a "ransom" price for all men (1 Tim 2:6). He was an ἀντίλυτρον (*antilytron*, "ransom price"). Satan had all of humankind in his clutches. He could rightly say that all men had disobeyed God's laws and that they had to pay the penalty. But then Jesus stepped in to pay the penalty for us and to set us free. We now belong to God! We could have only been redeemed by one who was not vulnerable to Satan's accusations himself. Jesus had no sin or else he could not have ransomed us.

3:6 No one who lives in him keeps on sinning. No one who continues to sin has either seen him or known him.

John is not claiming that Christians do not sin, for he has already said (1:8-10) that if we claim to be without sin, we are liars. The expression "who lives in him," literally means "abides, or remains" in him. This statement was not intended to mean that we do not sin; it means we do not live a life of sin. See notes on verses 8-9 later. John wants to make it perfectly clear that the gnostic idea of sin was not in keeping with what had been revealed from the Savior. **No one who continues to live a life of sin has either seen him or known[4] him.**

---

[4]"Known," translated from ἔγνωκεν, perfect indicative of the verb γινώσκω.

3:7 Dear children, do not let anyone lead you astray.
In this very grave warning, John uses the word "little children." Perhaps he wants them to realize that he both loves them (for this is a very endearing word) and that he wants to impress upon them their fallibility in the face of serious temptation to follow new and fanciful doctrines. Even in our own day, there must be constant vigilance for those who would teach error. As we have tried to impress, many of the teachings of the Gnostics have arisen in different situations throughout the ages, and we have many of them in such new heresies as the New Age movement. The apostle Paul gave serious warnings not unlike those of John. To the elders (the leaders and shepherds of the flock of Christians) Paul warned, "I know that after I leave, savage wolves will come in among you and will not spare the flock. *Even from your own number* [emphasis mine] men will arise and distort the truth in order to draw away disciples after them. So be on your guard! Remember that for three years I never stopped warning each of you night and day with tears" (Acts 20:29-31). None of us is totally out of the devil's reach. Without constant protection from our Father and Jesus his Son, we could all fall into the hands of Satan.

He who does what is right is righteous, just as he is righteous.
Living right, or righteously, is living according to law or not missing the mark. John's first statement here is really self-explanatory. It seems, however, that John is emphasizing this great truth because some were in danger of being led astray by the gnostic teachings that sin was not a reality. They needed to be told that forgiveness and cleansing from sin are vitally important to all of them. Paul faced this same problem, and he deals with it in Romans 6:1ff. He asked them "Shall we go

---

This is the verb form of the word from which "Gnostic" comes, and John must be making a pointed argument against the Gnostics in this statement about sin. One could not be a "knowing one" and continue to live in sin.

on sinning so that grace may increase?" to which he answered, "By no means!" Whether he was dealing here with gnostic teachers or someone else who was trying to minimize the terribleness of sin, we do not know. Both John and Paul deal very forthrightly about the terrible consequences of sin and how we must avoid sin. **He who does what is right is righteous, just as he is righteous.** Jesus is undoubtedly the one who is righteous. John uses the same emphatic word as he did in verse 3 to refer to Jesus.[5] Associating (or, fellowshiping) with Jesus will assure us the right example and the appropriate standard by which to build our lives.

3:8 He who does what is sinful is of the devil, because the devil has been sinning from the beginning.

We have seen that sin is incompatible with Christ, and Christians should therefore avoid it. A second reason why we should avoid sin is because of its origin. It is not merely "missing the mark." It puts us into the "family of Satan." The devil is the originator of sin; he is the father of sin. He evidently was disobedient to God from the very beginning. There are a number of statements in the Scripture that indicate that Satan was a rebellious, fallen angel. John pushes the time of his rebellious fall to an early point: **from the beginning.** The devil has been sinning[6] from the beginning; and ever since that time it has been the very nature of the devil to be a sinner.

The reason the Son of God appeared was to destroy the devil's work.

The mission of Jesus in his first coming was to destroy sin

---

[5]In verse 3, he uses the phrase καθὼς ἐκεῖνος ἁγνός ἐστιν (*kathōs ekeinos hagnos estin*, "just as he himself is holy") to show that we are holy because he is holy and has made us holy. In this verse he uses identical construction, καθὼς ἐκεῖνος δίκαιός ἐστιν (*kathos ekeinos dikaios estin*, "just as he himself is righteous") to show that we are righteous because he is righteous.

[6]"Has been sinning," from the Greek word ἁμαρτάνει (*hamartanei*, "is sinning"), a verb form that signifies the idea of a continuing activity of sin.

and the devil. Paul says that Christ "must reign until he has put all enemies under his feet. The last enemy to be destroyed is death" (1 Cor 15:25-26). Even though death is still present among us, Paul assures us that Jesus has actually destroyed death through his resurrection. We indicated earlier that Jesus' first coming was as a savior and his second coming will be as a judge. This is certainly true so far as the devil is concerned.

3:9 No one who is born of God will continue to sin, because God's seed remains in him; he cannot go on sinning, because he has been born of God.

Born of God is from the word γεγεννημένος (*gegennēmenos*, a perfect passive participle, meaning "has already been born of God"). Being a perfect tense, it signifies that the Christian has already been born of God and remains in that condition. And the expression **will continue to sin** is a continuous present tense, indicating that one born of God will not continue living a life of sin. Again, it is not intended to suggest that the one born of God will never sin or make a mistake; it means that he will not live a life that is characterized by sin.

3:10 This is how we know who the children of God are and who the children of the devil are: Anyone who does not do what is right is not a child of God; nor is anyone who does not love his brother.

How do we know who the children of God are and who the children of the devil are? Very simply: by their fruits. Those who continue living a life of sin cannot be children of God. And those who do not love their brothers are not children of God. There is an interesting inference that we might draw from John's discussion. One would assume, from the number of times John discusses it, that the Gnostics may not have believed in or practiced love for their brothers. We read that they were a very self-centered people who believed that they were better than others. After all, they divided people into three categories: sinners, ordinary Christians (who had not received the special gift of spiritual knowledge), and the gnostic Christians (who had this special knowledge which separated them from all others). Is it possible that this also included not loving their brothers?

D. LOVE ONE ANOTHER (3:11-24)

[11]This is the message you heard from the beginning: We should love one another. [12]Do not be like Cain, who belonged to the evil one and murdered his brother. And why did he murder him? Because his own actions were evil and his brother's were righteous. [13]Do not be surprised, my brothers, if the world hates you. [14]We know that we have passed from death to life, because we love our brothers. Anyone who does not love remains in death. [15]Anyone who hates his brother is a murderer, and you know that no murderer has eternal life in him.

[16]This is how we know what love is: Jesus Christ laid down his life for us. And we ought to lay down our lives for our brothers. [17]If anyone has material possessions and sees his brother in need but has no pity on him, how can the love of God be in him? [18]Dear children, let us not love with words or tongue but with actions and in truth. [19]This then is how we know that we belong to the truth, and how we set our hearts at rest in his presence [20]whenever our hearts condemn us. For God is greater than our hearts, and he knows everything.

[21]Dear friends, if our hearts do not condemn us, we have confidence before God [22]and receive from him anything we ask, because we obey his commands and do what pleases him. [23]And this is his command: to believe in the name of his Son, Jesus Christ, and to love one another as he commanded us. [24]Those who obey his commands live in him,

COLLEGE PRESS NIV COMMENTARY

**and he in them. And this is how we know that he lives in us:
We know it by the Spirit he gave us.**

These next fourteen verses give us one of the most powerful expressions of love that you will find. John returns to the
role of love as proof that we are walking in the light. He
reminds them that this is a central part of the message they
had received in the beginning.

**3:11 This is the message you heard from the beginning: We
should love one another.**

This part of his message to them is connected with the previous statements about who is a son of righteousness and who
is a son of the devil. He begins verse 11 with the words, ὅτι
αὕτη (*hoti hautē*, "because this" is the message from the beginning), indicating the direct relation of the two thoughts. In
other words, it is because it is connected to the message from
the beginning, *then* **we should love one another.**

**3:12 Do not be like Cain, who belonged to the evil one and
murdered his brother. And why did he murder him?
Because his own actions were evil and his brother's were
righteous.**

When we fulfill this commandment to love one another,
we must be careful that our lives are not like that of Cain (see
Gen 4:2-16) who committed the first murder by killing his
own brother. John is showing that Cain did not love his brother, as evidenced by his cold-blooded murder of Abel. The situation between them arose because the two brothers had
offered sacrifices to God; God accepted Abel's offering but
rejected Cain's offering. We are not certain why Abel's was
acceptable but Cain's wasn't. John said the reason he murdered Abel was because **his own actions were evil and his
brother's were righteous.** What he did that his actions were
evil, we do not know. Was it because Cain offered from the
produce of the field while Abel offered a blood sacrifice from

his flocks? Was it because only Abel offered his sacrifice "by faith" (Heb 11:4)? We are not told, but for some reason Cain was rejected because he did not properly obey God. John used the illustration of Cain to show the depth of love that we should have for our brothers. Cain's hatred for his brother illustrates a life without righteousness.

3:13 Do not be surprised, my brothers, if the world hates you.

It is likely that the Christians of this time were enduring hatred and mistreatment by those "on the cutting edge," as it were, of Christian thinking. These Gnostics were probably making fun of the other Christians for not going along with their false teaching. Certainly the "world" was rejecting this new belief called the "Way," and John is warning them not to be discouraged. Even in our day, we should not "be surprised if the world hates" us; neither should those of John's day have been surprised if they hated the Christians. The same situation exists in our world (and in *their* world) as existed with Cain and Abel. If the world is evil and God's children are righteous, why should it be surprising that the world hated them?

3:14 We know that we have passed from death to life, because we love our brothers. Anyone who does not love remains in death.

John is showing in these verses that love is the *evidence of* righteousness, not the *basis of* spiritual living. Earlier John stated that to be righteous, one must obey the commandments (commands) of God. Now, he equates righteousness with loving one's brother. In verse 14, hating one's brother is identified as murder. In the Sermon on the Mount Jesus says the same thing: "You have heard that it was said to the people long ago, 'Do not murder, and anyone who murders will be subject to judgment.' But I tell you that anyone who is angry with his brother will be subject to judgment," and ultimately this can lead to hell (Matt 5:21-22).

90

COLLEGE PRESS NIV COMMENTARY

COLLEGE PRESS NIV COMMENTARY

3:15 Anyone who hates his brother is a murderer, and you know that no murderer has eternal life in him.
Hatred of our brother is identified as murder, and murderers have no place in heaven. This is altogether reasonable, because the one who destroys life has set himself against eternal life.

3:16 This is how we know what love is: Jesus Christ laid down his life for us. And we ought to lay down our lives for our brothers.
This verse is obviously a comparison, in John's mind, of Cain and Christ. Cain showed his feelings by murdering his brother. Jesus shows his love to us by laying down his life for us. Here John gives us a definition of "love." He defines it by giving an example of what it does. We know love, he says, because **Jesus . . . laid down his life for us.** Love takes place when we become "other-centered" rather than "self-centered." In his Gospel, John quotes Jesus as saying, "God so loved the world that he gave his one and only[7] Son, that whoever believes in him shall not perish but have eternal life" (John 3:16). The extent of Jesus' love is also seen in John 15:12-13, "My command is this: Love each other as I have loved you. Greater love has no one than this, that he lay down his life for his friends." And Jesus demonstrated the power of his love in laying down his life for all of his friends (or, disciples). Marshall has this comment, "It [this passage in 1 John 3:16] indicates that one is prepared to give up one's own life in order that others may live. Love means saying 'No' to one's own life so that somebody else may live. Finally, it should be noted that the laying down of life is done for the benefit of the other person."[8] John then makes this action of Jesus even

---

[7]Or, "God's only begotten son," from τὸν υἱὸν τὸν μονογενῆ (*ton huion ton monogenē*, the son of him, the only begotten," or "the only begotten son of him."
[8]Marshall, *The Epistles of John*, p. 193.

more personal to his readers by saying that we too should lay down our lives for each other.

3:17 If anyone has material possessions and sees his brother in need but has no pity on him, how can the love of God be in him?

John now illustrates the extent to which our love should reach. It is a demanding requirement! In our day (especially in highly developed nations like America) most of us have far more than we actually need to sustain ourselves. John demands that we lay down part of that which we have to give to a needy brother. This is how κοινωνία (*koinōnia,* "fellowship, oneness") should work in our lives. The early church "shared everything they had" (Acts 4:32) with each other. We certainly realize that this was a special situation when people had come from throughout the world, were converted to Jesus Christ, and stayed on in Jerusalem to learn more about this new "Way" they had just found. Certainly there is a kind of spiritual practicality that we must be able to use in applying this to our lives. May God forbid that we use this "spiritual practicality" inappropriately for our own selfish gain, but each person should examine his/her life to decide how we apply this "definition" of love to our own spiritual lives.

3:18 Dear children, let us not love with words or tongue but with actions and in truth.

This brief section shows how we can have assurance that we are acceptable to our Lord. Our love must not be merely for show. We must do more than just "talk a good love." I knew a farmer many years ago who could "talk a good crop" for the next year during the winter months. But when it came time to carry out his plans, they were not very successful. Many are this way with their love. They talk about and tell how great their love is. But it is only **love with words or tongue**, as John charges. We must put our love into action. Only then will it be love **in truth.**

3:19 This then is how we know that we belong to the truth, and how we set our hearts at rest in his presence 3:20 whenever our hearts condemn us. For God is greater than our hearts, and he knows everything.

Our love helps us to know whether we belong to the truth. John tells us that when we know that our hearts condemn us, our love is insufficient. Since God is greater than our hearts, then he can know who we are and what we are. Let us not try to deceive God by having only a "love with words or tongue." God knows our hearts. We can **set our hearts at rest in his presence** if we are obedient to his command. We know that we "belong to the truth" when our consciences are at ease in his presence.

3:21 Dear friends, if our hearts do not condemn us, we have confidence before God

J.W Roberts gives a very good overview of verses 21-23. He writes, "As a conclusion to his second major part of the epistle, John mentions three things which seem unrelated to each other but which tie to the major themes of the epistle. First he expands the mention of the believer's confidence before God to include the answer to prayer (vss. 21, 22). Next, he combines the two themes of believing in Jesus as the Son of God and loving one another as the commandment of Christ (vs. 23). Lastly he confirms the fellowship of those who do the commandments by their having the Holy Spirit (vs. 24)."[9] In verse 19, John discusses "hearts at rest" and hearts that "condemn." If our hearts are in tune with God's heart, then our consciences are at rest. This is what John is saying here. If **our hearts do not condemn us,** then we are "in tune" with God and we have confidence before God. How can one have confidence before God when that heart is impure?

---

[9]Roberts, *The Letters of John*, p. 97.

3:22 and receive from him anything we ask, because we obey his commands and do what pleases him.

Although the impure, or pure, heart is a very important element of Christian living, this was not the major reason John mentions it here. He mentions it here to show the relationship we have with God. We **will receive from him anything we ask.** Why can we be confident that we will receive what we ask? **Because we obey his commands and do what pleases him.** God will be responsive to his children, and his true children will be obedient to him and will make him proud because we seek to please him. This is the essence of how we keep a clean conscience — to remain in his fellowship.

3:23 And this is his command: to believe in the name of his Son, Jesus Christ, and to love one another as he commanded us.

As if his readers have forgotten what his commands are, John tells them. God's command is singular: to believe Jesus Christ and to love one another. It would appear from John's statement that you can't have one without the other. Many in our world would have us believe that all that is necessary to be a good Christian is to just be filled with love for one another, but this is not what John is saying here or elsewhere. The love must be coupled with faith in Jesus Christ. It is not true that anyone who shows love for others is a Christian. Again, it should be emphasized that an idle, inactive faith can be a damnable thing to have. Faith, to be acceptable to God, has to be accompanied with works of obedience (see the first and last sentences of the book of Romans. James warns that even the "demons believe . . . and shudder" (James 2:19). So it is not enough to believe and do nothing about it. Nor can we have love without doing something. Love is one of the greatest motivators we have. You cannot truly love without demonstrating it. So, when John summarizes the meaning of the commands of Jesus, he is stressing the deepest involvement with the Lord that we can have.

3:24 Those who obey his commands live in him, and he in them.

One of John's favorite phrases (and certainly, one of Paul's) is "in him." Both of these apostles use this to describe the relationship that we have with Jesus. We are "in him" and he is "in us," as we can see from the first part of this verse. It sounds like this is not possible, for how can I be "in him" and he be "in me" at the same time? This is another way of saying that if we have the proper relationship with Jesus, then we have a common identity. This language reminds us of John's use of such terms as "abide in him," the union and fellowship (*koinōnia*) that we share with Jesus. We are told in John's Gospel that "If anyone loves me, he will obey my teaching. My Father will love him and we will come to him and make our home with him. He who does not love me will not obey my teaching. These words you hear are not my own; they belong to the Father who sent me" (John 14:23-24). John insists that obedience to the commandments of God is the condition for having communion with him. This relationship was undoubtedly pointed to the Gnostics who said that it is impossible for man to come into a communion or direct fellowship with God. This was because God is spiritual and mankind is material.

And this is how we know that he lives in us: We know it by the Spirit he gave us.

How do we know that we have fellowship and communion with God? **We know it by the Spirit he gave us.** This is the same Spirit that Jesus promised he would send after he left his disciples. "But the Counselor, the Holy Spirit, whom the Father will send in my name, will teach you all things and will remind you of everything I have said to you" (John 14:26). God did not leave us alone when Jesus returned to heaven; we have the indwelling of the Holy Spirit.

1 JOHN 4

IV. TESTING THE SPIRITS/TRUSTING GOD
(4:1–5:12)

A. TESTING THE SPIRITS (4:1-6)

[1]Dear friends, do not believe every spirit, but test the spirits to see whether they are from God, because many false prophets have gone out into the world. [2]This is how you can recognize the Spirit of God: Every spirit that acknowledges that Jesus Christ has come in the flesh is from God, [3]but every spirit that does not acknowledge Jesus is not from God. This is the spirit of the antichrist, which you have heard is coming and even now is already in the world.

[4]You, dear children, are from God and have overcome them, because the one who is in you is greater than the one who is in the world. [5]They are from the world and therefore speak from the viewpoint of the world, and the world listens to them. We are from God, and whoever knows God listens to us; but whoever is not from God does not listen to us. This is how we recognize the Spirit[a] of truth and the spirit of falsehood.

[a]6 Or *spirit*

Here, John returns to his arguments contained in 2:18-27 in which he is attacking the false prophets and their teachings, namely the Gnostics. Now, however, he is instructing his readers on how they should treat false teachers and how the false teachers can be identified.

John introduces a new phrase (for him) in these first six verses. He uses the expression "of God"[1] seven times. It is obvious that he is making a strong argument for the source of his teachings: they are "of" or "from God" himself. This is in contradistinction to the source of the heretics' teaching. John would argue, in keeping with his previous discussions, that the teachings of the heretics came from the devil, who has been a liar from the beginning.

4:1 Dear friends,

Again, John uses the word ἀγαπητοί (*agapētoi*, "beloved" or "dearly beloved") in reference to his readers. "Dearly beloved" or "beloved" would seem to be a better rendition of the word than the NIV use of **Dear friends**. The NIV translation seems to be more limiting, while "dearly beloved" is a stronger translation.

do not believe every spirit, but test the spirits to see whether they are from God, because many false prophets have gone out into the world.

The Old Testament tells of many false prophets who roamed the world. For example, there were the prophets of Baal and Asherah during the days of Elijah and other later prophets. The Israelites were told to test the prophets. So, in New Testament days, there were also many false teachers trying to lead the Christians astray, not the least of which were the Gnostics. John is warning that they "test the spirits," or teachers, to see whether they are from God. Deuteronomy lays down two tests for determining whether prophets were true or false. "You may say to yourselves, 'How can we know when a message has not been spoken by the LORD?' If what a prophet proclaims in the name of the LORD does not take

---

[1]This phrase "of God" is expressed by two different but similar phrases: one is the use of the prepositional phrase ἐκ τοῦ θεοῦ (*ek tou theou*, literally, "out of [i.e., originating from] God"), and τοῦ θεοῦ, which also means "of" or "from God."

place or come true, that is a message the LORD has not spoken. That prophet has spoken presumptuously. Do not be afraid of him" (Deut 18:21-22). The two tests recommended in Deuteronomy are: (1) "if the word does not come to pass or come true;" and (2) "even if the word which the prophet speaks comes true, yet if he tries to lead his hearers astray to serve other gods, he is a false prophet" (Deut 13:1-5).[2] No spirit should be accepted until it has been tested and proved by God's Holy Spirit. The Holy Spirit is the final witness during the Christian age, for Jesus promised that he would come and "teach you all things" and "will remind you of everything I have said to you" (see John 14:26).

This warning from John probably indicates that some of the Christians he is addressing have been listening to some of the false prophets without "testing" them.[3] Not only in John's day, but also in our own time, we must be on guard against false prophets, for they still exist among us. We must "test the spirits" to see if they are from God. These gnostic teachers must not be accepted unless they have been tested.

4:2 This is how you can recognize the Spirit of God: Every spirit that acknowledges that Jesus Christ has come in the flesh is from God,

This is not the only identifying mark of a true prophet or

---

[2]See Bruce, *The Epistles of John*, p. 104.

[3]*The Expositor's Greek Testament* has this statement in a footnote: "The apostle has just said that the Spirit begets in us the assurance that God abideth in us. And this suggests a warning. The Cerinthian heresy also had much to say about 'the spirit.' It boasted a larger spirituality. Starting with the philosophical postulate of an irreconcilable antagonism between matter and spirit, it denied the possibility of the Incarnation and drew a distinction between Jesus and the Christ . . . . Its spirit was not 'the Spirit of truth' but 'a spirit of error,' and thus the necessity arises of 'proving the spirits'. δοκιμάζειν, of 'proving' or 'testing' a coin (νόμισμα). If it stood the test, it was δόκιμον [or, 'approved,' or 'genuine'] (*cf.* 2 Cor. x. 18); if it was found counterfeit (κίβδηλον) it was ἀδόκιμον [or, 'unreal' or 'worthless'] (*cf.* 1 Cor. ix. 27; 2 Cor. xiii. 5-7)." W. Robertson Nicoll, editor, *The Expositor's Greek Testament*, Vol. 5 (New York: Hodder and Stoughton, 1922), p. 189.

the teaching of the Spirit of God. This is only in reference to the false teaching that John is addressing, Gnosticism, or specifically, Docetism. There were other elements of the gnostic philosophy that would be contrary to the teachings from God; this is the one addressed here. Some commentators are convinced that the Christians in John's day may have been required to make a confession of his/her belief in the physical nature of Jesus. This may be based on the use of the expression πᾶν πνεῦμα ὃ ὁμολογεῖ Ἰησοῦν Χριστὸν (*pan pneuma ho homologei Iēsoun Christon*, "every spirit who confesses Jesus Christ") in this verse. The emphasis is upon the words *ho homologei*, which mean "who confesses." The NIV translation is "who acknowledges," but the more accurate rendition is probably "who confesses." From this use of the word "confess" some assume that a confession was expected of those who accepted Jesus. I have no specific opinion on this, but it certainly is a possibility. It was not long after this period of time that the Apostles' Creed, in its earliest forms, came to be recited by the early Christians.

Recognizing the earthly nature of Jesus, as well as his divine nature, begins to take on a very important element of faith. In a little over two centuries, the first Nicene Council would be called for the purpose of clarifying the nature of Jesus. It is impossible for us to determine with exactness when this came to be one of the divisive elements of Christian faith. But, John declares here that this is the way we know if a spirit, or prophet, has come from God: if it **acknowledges** [or, confesses] **that Jesus has come in the flesh.**

4:3 but every spirit that does not acknowledge Jesus is not from God.

Earlier, we noted that John often restates an argument with a negative statement. This is another instance of this aspect of his writing style. In order to assure that his readers would not misunderstand his admonition, he states the same truth in reverse form. The acknowledgement, or confession, here is a parallel to the previous clause, and involves a confession that Jesus "has come in the flesh." The incarnation (coming in the flesh) of Jesus is, therefore, one of the fundamental principles of our faith in God. The incarnation of Jesus certainly presupposes the preexistence of Jesus, that is, the eternal existence of Jesus (see John 1:1ff; 1 John 1:1ff). I recall hearing a professor of mine say, "I believe in what the virgin birth stands for (by this, he meant the coming of Christ into the world), but I do not believe that Jesus was literally born of a virgin." We have no right to take part of God's truth and not accept *all* of it. In our own day of rationalizing the Bible to our own desires, we have the same commission that John gave his readers: we must accept the fact that Jesus came in the flesh and that he was the only begotten Son of God.

This is the spirit of the antichrist, which you have heard is coming and even now is already in the world.
    Again, John identifies who, or what, the antichrist is: it is one who denies the incarnation, or the fleshly appearance of God, in our lives and in the world. Not only does he declare that the antichrist is coming, but it **is already in the world.** The antichrist is personified in "those who went out from" these Christians John is addressing. It is the Gnostic who denies the physical reality of Jesus!

4:4 You, dear children, are from God and have overcome them,
    The expression "dear children" in the Greek is merely τεκνία (*teknia*), "children," not "dear children." This is an attempt on the part of the NIV, and certainly not incorrect in its intention, of showing the very special relationship John had with these Christians. He declares that they are **from God.** And you **have overcome them.** "Them" undoubtedly refers to those who had accepted the false teachings of the Gnostics.

because the one who is in you is greater than the one who is in the world.

The one who is in you, without question, refers to the Holy Spirit, or the Spirit of God. The gender in this expression in the Greek has changed from the neuter gender in earlier references to "spirit" to the masculine gender, referring to the Holy Spirit. This inner power provided by the Holy Spirit enables us to be more successful in our struggle against the devil and his false teachings. Furthermore, John asserts that **the one who is in you is greater than the one who is in the world.** The world has not been given the indwelling of the Holy Spirit, for it is only given to those who were baptized into Jesus (see Acts 2:38). Without the indwelling of the Holy Spirit, they are powerless to fight against evil and false teaching. When people accept Jesus into their lives and obey his commands, they become a distinctly different people, or as Peter says, they become "a chosen people, a royal priesthood, a holy nation, a people belonging to God" (1 Pet 2:9).

4:5 They are from the world and therefore speak from the viewpoint of the world, and the world listens to them.

These false teachers have gone out into the world. John insists that they are a part of this world. Hence **they speak from the viewpoint of the world.** Their success in spreading their heresy is undoubtedly because they speak the language of the world and the world understands them. We should remember that our language tells others who and what we are. When Peter and John astonished their listeners with what they said, "they were astonished and took note that these men had been with Jesus" (Acts 4:13). "Being with Jesus" makes a difference in what we say, how we act, and what kind of person we are.

4:6 We are from God, and whoever knows God listens to us; but whoever is not from God does not listen to us. This is

**how we recognize the Spirit of truth and the spirit of false-
hood.**

Since we are **from God,** others who are also from God will
know us by how we act and what we say. They will know that
God listens to us because God listens to his own. Those who
are not "from God" will not know us nor understand us. This
being true, if God is speaking to us through his Holy Spirit
and through the revelation given to us, we will know it
because we know God. Those heretics John is discussing will
not know what the truth is because they do not know what
God speaks. They are not from God. There is a sort of parallel between John and these heretics. The Gnostics believed
that they had received a special gift of knowledge from God
that made them more exclusive than others who were in the
Way. The Christians had received the Holy Spirit of God and
He speaks to us through revelation. But, that is as far as the
parallel goes — that each group (the Christians and the
Gnostics) had received a special gift from God.

B. GOD'S LOVE AND OUR LOVE (4:7-21)

[7]**Dear friends, let us love one another, for love comes
from God. Everyone who loves has been born of God and
knows God.** [8]**Whoever does not love does not know God,
because God is love.** [9]**This is how God showed his love
among us: He sent his one and only Son**[a] **into the world that
we might live through him.** [10]**This is love: not that we loved
God, but that he loved us and sent his Son as an atoning sacrifice for**[b] **our sins.** [11]**Dear friends, since God so loved us, we
also ought to love one another.** [12]**No one has ever seen God;
but if we love one another, God lives in us and his love is
made complete in us.**

[13]**We know that we live in him and he in us, because he
has given us of his Spirit.** [14]**And we have seen and testify**

that the Father has sent his Son to be the Savior of the world. ¹⁵If anyone acknowledges that Jesus is the Son of God, God lives in him and he in God. ¹⁶And so we know and rely on the love God has for us.

God is love. Whoever lives in love lives in God, and God in him. ¹⁷In this way, love is made complete among us so that we will have confidence on the day of judgment, because in this world we are like him. ¹⁸There is no fear in love. But perfect love drives out fear, because fear has to do with punishment. The one who fears is not made perfect in love.

¹⁹We love because he first loved us. ²⁰If anyone says, "I love God," yet hates his brother, he is a liar. For anyone who does not love his brother, whom he has seen, cannot love God, whom he has not seen. ²¹And he has given us this command: Whoever loves God must also love his brother.

^a9 Or *his only begotten Son*   ^b10 Or *as the one who would turn aside his wrath, taking away*

Already in this epistle, John has addressed "love" in some of the strongest language possible. In 2:1-11, he discusses love from the point of view of its being a new command. In 3:11-21, he shows how important it is for us to love one another. In 4:7-21, he discusses God's love and our love. He shows how love is a Godlike trait, emphasizes our love as we try to become like God in our practice of love.

4:7 Dear friends, let us love one another, for love comes from God. Everyone who loves has been born of God and knows God.

Again, the NIV has weakened the force of the first word of this text by translating it **Dear friends**. As we have indicated before, the force of this word is "beloved," or "dearly beloved." **Let us** is a hortatory subjunctive, and it is a strong encouragement to move forward. "Let us" really is a statement that urges his listeners to do as he plans to do, that is **love one**

another. Often, "loving one another" could be a translation of *philos* or *phileō*, but here John uses the stronger word *agapaō* from which we get the noun *agapē*. Why should we Christians love one another? Because **love comes from God.** If we carry the theme John is emphasizing of the family relation of God the Father with his children, Christians, we could say that love is a family characteristic. We love because our Father before us loves. John further stresses this point when he says that **Everyone who loves has been born of God and knows God.** Two striking statements here again attack the gnostic beliefs: first, we have been "born of God." Second, we "know God." Both of these statements would run counter to the beliefs of the Gnostics, for they did not believe that "ordinary Christians," like those being addressed by John had either of these characteristics. We will say more about being "born of God" in 5:18-19. You are encouraged to turn and read those verses in connection with this theme of John. How can we "know" God? Through his revelation of himself to us through Jesus Christ and confirmed to us by the revelation of the Holy Spirit to us in Scripture.

4:8 Whoever does not love does not know God, because God is love.

The expression **does not know God**[4] makes it obligatory upon everyone who claims God to love not only him, but also his children. Jesus uses the same Greek word in Matthew 7:23 when he said to those claiming to know God, "I never knew [ἔγνων, *egnōn*] you."

Here, again, John uses the language of the Gnostics in saying whoever does not love does not *know* God. There is no specific object of the love mentioned, just **whoever does not**

---

[4]Lenski renders this Greek expression, οὐκ ἔγνω τὸν θεόν (*ouk egnō ton theon*), as "did not know God." This would have the force of saying "never did know God, because it is not in the nature of one in God's family to know God if he has not loved God."

love does not know God. The reason for this all-encompassing statement about love is **because God is love.** If God truly
is love, then not-loving would be proof that we are ungodly,
or ungodlike. This love that God *is* encompasses intelligence,
intention, comprehension, and understanding, because to
love in the manner that God is (that is, *agapē*, which we have
already defined in previous pages) is not necessarily a love of
passion, but a love of intention. We can be commanded to
love in the manner that God loves. We can have compassion,
concern for others' best, benevolence, and all the wide meanings that love really is. When one first hears the expression,
"God is love," this sounds so simple and so easy to understand. But, in fact it is one of the most sublime, most inclusive, most all-encompassing traits we can have. Lenski wrote,
"God is love. Love as well as life reveals its presence by its
acts. In 3:1 it is the Father's gift that makes us his children."[5]

**4:9 This is how God showed his love among us: He sent his one
and only Son[6] into the world that we might live through him.**

What a way to demonstrate love! Only when a person has
had to give up a son (or daughter) through death can we even
approximate the greatness of the gift God gave. When we
magnify the pain by recognizing the extent of the pain and
humiliation that Jesus, God's Son, experienced and realize
what a worthless people we humans were for God to sacrifice
his Son for us, we can begin to realize something of the greatness of the sacrifice of God. No one can ever question the
magnitude of the suffering of God until it is realized what a
sacrifice it was. God manifested his love "in us," or "among
us,"[7] which signifies the overt way that God performed this

---

[5]Lenski, *The Epistles of Peter, John, and Jude,* p. 500.
[6]Or, τὸν υἱὸν αὐτοῦ τὸν μονογενῆ (*ton huion autou ton monogenē*) can be
equally correctly translated as "his only begotten son."
[7]Ἐν τούτῳ ἐφανερώθη ἡ ἀγάπη τοῦ θεοῦ ἐν ἡμῖν (*en touto ephanerōthē hē
agapē tou theou en hēmin,* "in this the love of God was made manifest in
us"). Ἐν ἡμῖν is translated by the NIV as "among us." This is an accurate

great demonstration of his love for us. He did it on the cross, with all of its shame and sorrow. This is in fulfillment of the prophecy, "He was despised and rejected by men, a man of sorrows, and familiar with suffering. Like one from whom men hide their faces he was despised, and we esteemed him not" (Isa 53:3). The sacrifice of Jesus on the cross was not a pretty thing. The American justice system seeks to assure that the death penalty will not suggest cruel and inhumane treatment. The Roman cross was the epitome of inhumane treatment: all of this because God wanted to show his love for us.

So, God sent his Son openly to all the world to give himself as a sacrifice for our sins, because he loved us. Not only did God send his Son to demonstrate his love, but also **that we might live through him.** This is not some kind of a future life that God provides. It is an immediate gift. We can be possessors of eternal life right here and now! This life is in harmony with the truly spiritual order of things! John often speaks of eternal life in the present tense or as an already accomplished fact: see 5:11,13. This in no way is a guarantee of eternal life or that we can do nothing to lose what we already have. If we were to reject Jesus, we would lose what he has promised (see 5:11).

4:10 This is love: not that we loved God, but that he loved us and sent his Son as an atoning sacrifice for our sins.

True love comes not from humankind; true love comes from God. It all started with God loving us. Even when humanity turned their backs on God, he still loved them. God did not need humanity; humanity had rejected God from the very beginning, even in the Garden of Eden. From that time till now, we have been in need of God. His love was seen when he sent his Son to atone for our sins: He is the **atoning sacrifice**

---

way to translate the phrase and it provides us with a broader understanding of what happened. It was not done in a corner, but it was open and among the people.

for our sins. Marshall writes that "In this phrase we find the deepest meaning of the term 'love': love means forgiving the sins of the beloved and remembering them no more. This is what God has done for rebellious mankind: he pardons their sins against himself at his own cost. To remove this element from the biblical teaching on the nature of God's love is to water down the concept of love beyond measure."[8] In no way was Jesus a martyr. He was a sacrifice. He was a propitiation. He was an "atoning sacrifice."[9] If we start at our point of being to learn the true meaning of love, we will never understand it. We must start with God in order to understand it.

4:11 Dear friends, since God so loved us, we also ought to love one another.

To the "Dearly beloved," or **Dear friends,** John addresses some of the obligations or responsibilities that arise out of God's love for us. Good things rarely come to us apart from obligations. God's love for us places the responsibility, or "ought," for us to **love one another.** This "ought" in our lives comes at a high price. Christ has died for our sins, we have received the forgiveness of our sins, and now **we also ought to love one another.** This comes as an obligation to us, as is suggested by the verb ὀφείλομεν (*opheilomen,* "we ought").[10]

4:12 No one has ever seen God;

This kind of love is different from any kind of love we experience with our fellow human beings. We love people in our physical existence because we see them, we associate with

---

[8]Marshall, *The Epistles of John,* p. 215.

[9]Jesus was an atoning sacrifice. Ἱλασμὸν περὶ τῶν ἁμαρτιῶν ἡμῶν (*hilasmon peri tōn hamartiōn hēmōn*) literally refers to an expiation or propitiation (*hilasmon*), or a "sin-offering." God paid the ultimate price for our sins.

[10]This verb is in the first person plural, and it literally means that we are obligated, or we owe a debt. When God loved us, that put us in debt to him. See Arndt & Gingrich, *Greek-English Lexicon,* pp. 598-599, for a fuller discussion of this word.

them, and for some reason, we come to love them. John reminds us that this is a different kind of love. **No one has ever seen God**. How can we love someone whom we have not seen? This is a concept addressed several times in the Old Testament. Moses was allowed to see God's back side but was never allowed to see "God's face." John discusses this elsewhere. "No one has ever seen God, but God the One and Only [NIV fn: but the only Son], who is at the Father's side, has made him known" (John 1:18). There is a difference in the "invisibility" of God and the revelation of the incarnate Son. Jesus taught his disciples that if they had seen him, then they had seen the Father.

but if we love one another, God lives in us and his love is made complete in us.

How, then, is it possible for us to love God whom we have not seen? We love him because He has expressed his love to us through the gift of his Son. When we recognize the world that God has created and the wonderful blessings that come from him, this should produce in us a love for the Father. [I]f **we love each other, God lives in us and his love is made complete in us.** This is the answer to our question, "How is it possible for us to love God whom we have not seen?" We develop our love through loving our fellow Christians, and God lives in us. His love is made complete when we learn to love him with all of our hearts, souls, and minds. This is the essence of love.

4:13 We know that we live in him and he in us, because he has given us of his Spirit.

The Holy Spirit has been given to all Christians. Peter declared to the great crowds of people on the Day of Pentecost, "Repent and be baptized, every one of you, in the name of Jesus Christ for the forgiveness of your sins. And you will receive the gift of the Holy Spirit" (Acts 2:38). In chapter five (5:6ff), John appeals to three witnesses to the incarnation of Jesus — the Spirit, the water and the blood — which we will discuss in detail later. But the presence of the Holy Spirit in our lives is certifying that we live in him. The Holy Spirit has demonstrated himself to us in a number of ways: the presence of the Spirit with Jesus on earth, the baptism of the Holy Spirit (to the apostles and the household of Cornelius), the laying on of hands, and the gift of the Holy Spirit. It is the "gift" that John is speaking of here. The "gift" is actually the Holy Spirit himself; God gives us the indwelling of the Holy Spirit. He has **given us of his Spirit.** He dwells within us, and this testifies that God loves us and that God lives in us. The Spirit has worked in our lives also in the revelation of God to us through his (the Spirit's) work. Paul states that the Holy Spirit was a "deposit" or an "earnest" of what was to come: "Now it is God who has made us for this very purpose and has given us the Spirit as a deposit, guaranteeing what is to come" (2 Cor 5:5). I recently bought a new house. When the purchase was agreed upon, I was asked to give a "deposit," or a down payment to show that I really meant to buy the house. This is what Paul is saying. God has promised us a "heavenly dwelling" (see 2 Corinthians 5:1) and to guarantee that he would give what he has promised, he gave the Holy Spirit as a "deposit." So, we know that we live in him and he in us because of the deposit God made.

4:14 And we have seen and testify that the Father has sent his Son to be the Savior of the world.

This is another attack on Cerinthus and his gnostic followers. God's *incarnate* Son, which the Docetics denied, came to earth, suffered, died and arose from the dead to give us forgiveness of sins and eternal life. John repeats what he said at the outset of this letter, **we have seen and testify** that these things actually happened (see 1:1-2). To what is John testifying? To the fact that **the Father has sent his Son to be the Savior of the world.** Bear in mind that this attacks Cerinthus and his followers at the very root of their doctrines. If John's

statement is true, then the gnostic foundation falls. All of this
happened because *God loves us and gave his Son as our Savior.*

**4:15 If anyone acknowledges[11] that Jesus is the Son of God,
God lives in him and he in God.**
    John returns to an argument he began earlier in this chap-
ter (see verses 2 & 3). The docetic view that Jesus was not
born of the flesh is a persistent theme throughout this epistle.
This became an essential part of the early Christian's confession of his faith. As we have indicated earlier, it was not long
after these words were written that the earliest forms of the
Apostle's Creed began to emerge. Although this writer is not
in favor of creeds and creedal developments, one can understand why some of the early Christians felt the need to verbal-
ize, or confess, the articles of their faith. One who would confess his faith in the Sonship of Jesus would be responding to
the false teachings of the gnostic system. The reality of the
Sonship of Jesus guarantees that God abides[12] in the one who
makes this confession. Faith in Jesus' Sonship causes God to
live in the believer and the believer to be a part of God, or to
live in him.

4:16 And so we know and rely on the love God has for us.
    We have ample proof that John is telling us the truth. He
has witnessed with his own eyes and touched, and talked with
Jesus as a man; his fellow disciples (perhaps referred to when
John wrote "which we have heard" [1:1]) The "we" certainly
could include all of those who had witnessed the life of Jesus.
As we shall see in the next chapter, three witnesses, according
to the Law of Moses, were enough to determine truth. We

---

[11]The word from which "acknowledge" is translated is ὁμολογήσῃ
(*homologēsē*, "may confess"). This confession would be a basic part of that
confessor's belief system.
[12]The word "lives" comes from the word μένει (*menei*), which has the
force of taking up residence.

can, therefore, rely on John's message. We can know and rely on the love that God has for us.

God is love. Whoever lives in love lives in God, and God in him.

John again makes the broad, inclusive statement, **God is love.** Stott makes these comments regarding this statement: "It tells us not only that God loved, but that *God is love.* It is one thing, however, to know and believe *the love God has for us* and that *God is love*; it is another to 'live in love' ourselves. . . .The only way to love, as the only way to believe (v. 15) is by living in God and God in us."[13] John assures us that whenever we practice love for God and for our brothers, we live in God and God lives in us. This is a most sublime thought: to know that God abides in us.

4:17 In this way, love is made complete among us so that we will have confidence on the day of judgment, because in this world we are like him.

Only when we put our faith in God, and allow his love to permeate our lives can love be perfected, or made complete.[14] So, God's love can be made complete in us when we love. We can then develop a true confidence in our lives. We can have confidence that God has redeemed us through his Son, for it was his love that sent Jesus to die for us. We can then look to the Day of Judgment with confidence that our eternal life is secure.

4:18 There is no fear in love. But perfect love drives out fear, because fear has to do with punishment. The one who fears is not made perfect in love.

With this confidence we can then be beyond fear. This is

---

[13]Stott, *The Letters of John,* p. 170.

[14]"Made complete" comes from the verb τετελείωται, 3rd person perfect passive of the verb τελειόω (*teleioō*), which means to make complete or entire.

why John assures us that there is no fear in love: because our confidence in our salvation is made secure. He also assures us that fear comes in when punishment is involved, and punishment will not be involved in our lives when we have allowed perfect love to abide in us. He emphatically says, **the man who fears is not made perfect in love.** What is your level of faith and love? Has it allowed you to develop a confident life? We must all strive for that kind of faith and love that provides us with confidence.

4:19 We love because he first loved us.

Since "God is love," then he is the source of all love. This is in keeping with John's statement that **We love because he first loved us.** We would not have known love if God had not demonstrated it to us first. The more that we behold God's love, the more we will understand it and respond positively to it. As we grow in our relationship with God, we will appreciate his love more and will learn to express our love.

4:20 If anyone says, "I love God," yet hates his brother, he is a liar. For anyone who does not love his brother, whom he has seen, cannot love God, whom he has not seen.

True love requires that it be expressed to others. The greatest of all commandments was to "'Love the Lord your God with all your heart and with all your soul and with all your mind.' This is the first and greatest commandment. And the second is like it: 'Love your neighbor as yourself'" (Matt 22:37-38). Jesus made this well-known comment to one who asked what is the greatest commandment. This being true, we can see why Jesus placed such an importance on loving our brother and why we are liars if we claim to love God and yet do not love our fellowman. John then gives the reason for this, **For anyone who does not love his brother, whom he has seen, cannot love God, whom he has not seen.** We may deceive our fellowmen by claiming to love God without loving our brothers. There are many people in God's church who have terrible attitudes toward each other. They will mistreat a brother, despise a brother, fail to practice brotherly love, and yet sing great praises to God at the same time. John says that this is not possible. We are liars when we make that claim.

4:21 And he has given us this command: Whoever loves God must also love his brother.

In concluding this chapter, John makes one further appeal for loving our brothers. This final reminder to love our brothers is needed. Evidently, it was also needed for these Christians in John's time or he would not be emphasizing it so much. It is possible that all of the problems surrounding the false teaching spreading among them had also developed hatred and lack of genuine love within the body. As we have already emphasized, this commandment is needed today in the Lord's body. There are too many Christians who do not properly regard each other. This is not a suggestion from God; it is a command!

1 JOHN 5

C. FAITH IN THE SON OF GOD (5:1-5)

[1]Everyone who believes that Jesus is the Christ is born of God, and everyone who loves the father loves his child as well. [2]This is how we know that we love the children of God: by loving God and carrying out his commands. [3]This is love for God: to obey his commands. And his commands are not burdensome, [4]for everyone born of God overcomes the world. This is the victory that has overcome the world, even our faith. [5]Who is it that overcomes the world? Only he who believes that Jesus is the Son of God.

As John begins the fifth chapter, he starts with a moral and natural principle: the closeness of family. He goes back to a principle that he started in 4:7ff. This is the principle of God's family. In 4:7, he states that "everyone who loves has been born of God and knows God." He is not claiming that all one has to do to be in the family of God is to have love. Many people who are not in the family of God certainly have love. Jesus had said, "Unless a man is born of water and the Spirit, he cannot enter the kingdom of God" (John 3:5). There is ample and adequate demonstration in the Scripture to show that the new birth occurs when one is baptized in the name of Jesus. We shall not take the time nor space here to argue this. But, being born of God involves more than *just* loving. Loving God and brother is more than just an emotional experience, or even a "doing good" experience. John makes clear in 5:2, "This is how we know that we love the children of God: by loving God and carrying out his commands." Since God is the Father of the family and his very nature is love ("God is love," 4:16), then it is one of the family traits for us to love God and our brothers if we are a part of the family of God. This, I believe, is the nature of the argument that John is making in these first two verses.

5:1 Everyone who believes that Jesus is the Christ is born of God,

Again, John is excluding those of the docetic persuasion in the gnostic movement from being in the family of God. They must believe in the incarnation [or "the coming in the flesh"] of Jesus. In the next several generations from when John is writing, this will become a very important element of Christology. This will be discussed in more than one of the Ecumenical Councils to come.

and everyone who loves the father loves his child as well.

As we have indicated earlier, there was evidently some great need in the church of John's day for the Christians to love one another. Otherwise, why would he emphasize it so often? If love is one of the familial traits in God's family, then each of his children will love God and love the brothers and the sisters, in God's family. You cannot love God without loving your brother. You cannot have one without the other. John reminds us that the way for us to become children of God is (1) by loving God; and (2) by carrying out his commands. His commands can be known by listening to the revelation of the Spirit of God. He was sent to bear witness to the message being taught. J.W. Roberts wrote, "John is actually saying, then, that the one continuing to believe[1] that Jesus is the Christ (having become a Christian) continues to demonstrate by this that he has been

---

[1]Roberts indicates that the verb is in the perfect tense, which indicates that an action was begun earlier, becoming a Christian, and continues right up to the present (*The Letters of John*, p. 125).

begotten or is a child of God. Continuing in the status of a child of God depends on continued faith in Jesus."[2] C.H. Dodd suggests that the word "father" in verse one need not be capitalized, which is the case in the NIV translation, it is a "general principle that if you love the parent you will love the child. (It is not necessary to give the 'father' a capital letter, for the writer is enunciating a general maxim: love me, love my child; although, of course, in the application which he gives it the parent is God and the child the Christian man.) the conclusion we expect is: therefore if you love God you will love your fellow Christian)."[3]

5:2 This is how we know that we love the children of God: by loving God and carrying out his commands.

But, how can we know that we are loving the children of God? Not everyone is lovable in nature, and sometimes it is difficult for us to love someone. How, for example, can we love one who does us or our society wrong? John gives us an answer: **by loving God and carrying out his commands.** So it is not a blind or empty kind of love; it involves loving God first, for Jesus said that this was the first and greatest commandment (Matt 22:34-40).

5:3 This is love for God: to obey his commands.

The kind of love that God expects from us is an obedient love. This should not surprise us, for Jesus is quoted by John as saying, "If you love me, you will obey what I command" (John 14:15). And, "Whoever has my commands and obeys them, he is the one who loves me. He who loves me will be loved by my Father, and I too will love him and show myself to him" (John 14:21). And, further he even calls us his friends if we obey him, "You are my friends if you do what I command" (John 15:14).

---

[2]Ibid., pp. 126-127.
[3]C.H. Dodd, *The Johannine Epistles* (New York: Harper & Brothers, 1946), pp. 124-125.

John is interested here in showing the continuing relationship with Christ. Loving our brothers is not only a command, but it is an "ought" that is bound on Christians. As we have said before, one cannot command the emotional type of love, but the kind of love that represents God can be commanded.

And his commands are not burdensome,
We are to obey the commands of God. John insists that **his commands are not burdensome.** I like the comments that Lenski makes to this, "Is it a burden to believe in the Son of God who died in expiation of our sins (2:2; 3:23; 4:10)? There is no greater joy than this confidence and trust. Is it a burden to be called one of God's children (3:1), children of him who is love (4:8, 16), and for the love of him who first loved us (4:10) to love him and thus also his children even as he loves us, and as they love us? Can there be any greater joy than to stand in this circle of love, to have this love poured out upon us, to be warmed into answering love by this love? No; his commandments are not burdensome!"[4] There is nothing that needs to be added to this. No, it is not burdensome. How can it be burdensome to respond to God's love?

5:4 for everyone born of God overcomes the world. This is the victory that has overcome the world, even our faith.
John now returns to one of the central arguments of this epistle: how to overcome the world, which includes overcoming the Gnostics' teaching that Jesus was not born of the flesh. God gives us the victory in Christ. Or, to express it more in the language of John, God *has already* given us the victory through Christ. When we are born again, at that moment we are given the victory. John is not teaching a salvation that cannot be lost. We can lose the victory by denying him who gave us the victory, namely, Jesus Christ. It is our faith that gives us the victory! As if we didn't get it the first

---

[4]Lenski, *The Epistles of Peter, John, and Jude*, pp. 520-521.

time, John repeats this truth, "Who is it that overcomes the world? Only he who believes that Jesus is the Son of God." For as long as I can remember, these statements have been some of the most awe-inspiring statements I know. Think of it! Our faith can and has overcome the world! All of Satan's dominion — the world — is under the power of him for whom we have dedicated our lives.

5:5 Who is it that overcomes the world? Only he who believes that Jesus is the Son of God.

In the opening verses of this chapter, John has suggested three things that characterize the children of God:

1) Those who have faith in the incarnation of Jesus Christ,
2) Those who love God and their brothers, and
3) Those who are obedient to the commands of God.

He concluded his characterization of God's children by saying, **Only he who believes that Jesus is the Son of God** will overcome the world. This is a bridge statement between what has gone before and what comes next.

D. THE THREE WITNESSES (5:6-12)

[6]This is the one who came by water and blood — Jesus Christ. He did not come by water only, but by water and blood. And it is the Spirit who testifies, because the Spirit is the truth. [7]For there are three that testify: [8]the[a] Spirit, the water and the blood; and the three are in agreement. [9]We accept man's testimony, but God's testimony is greater because it is the testimony of God, which he has given about his Son. [10]Anyone who believes in the Son of God has this testimony in his heart. Anyone who does not believe God has made him out to be a liar, because he has not believed the testimony God has given about his Son. [11]And this is the testimony: God has given us eternal life, and this life is in

his Son. [12]He who has the Son has life; he who does not have
the Son of God does not have life.

ª7,8 Late manuscripts of the Vulgate *testify in heaven: the Father, the Word
and the Holy Spirit, and these three are one.* [8]*And there are three that testify
on earth: the* (not found in any Greek manuscript before the sixteenth
century)

The subject addressed by John here is that of "witnesses"
or "testimony." He began his epistle with the subject of "witnesses" and now he is bringing it to a close with the same subject. He began by discussing, "That which was from the beginning, which we have heard, which we have seen with our eyes,
which we have looked at and our hands have touched" (1 John
1:2). He has declared that "we" (whoever the "we" refers to)
have truly witnessed the historical Jesus, the one who has
become incarnate. What greater witness can one have than to
have heard, seen, and touched, that which has existed from
the beginning: the "we" may be the original twelve apostles,
some of the Christians to whom John was writing, or another
group which make up the "we." I have stated earlier that it is
my view that the "we" were those who originally saw him in
the flesh, perhaps the apostles. For John's argument, it really
does not make a great difference, for if there were three or
more, this satisfied the legal requirements of the Law of
Moses to make a declaration. Moses had declared many years
before, "One witness is not enough to convict a man accused
of any crime or offense he may have committed. A matter
must be established by the testimony of two or three witnesses" (Deut 19:15). Jesus was evidently alluding to this when he
was discussing how we should treat matters with our brothers.
"If your brother sins against you, go and show him his fault,
just between the two of you. If he listens to you, you have
won your brother over. But if he will not listen, take one or
two others along, so that 'every matter may be established by
the testimony of two or three witnesses.' If he refuses to listen
to them, tell it to the church; and if he refuses to listen even

to the church, treat him as you would a pagan or a tax collector" (Matt 18:15-17).

John refers to multiple "witnesses" to Jesus' reality in the opening verses of this epistle. And, in the verses we are currently looking at, he is evidently conscious of the three witnesses.[5] As noted in the footnote, some of these words are not in the NIV and other more modern translations, because they do not appear in some of the earliest manuscripts. Marshall has a good insight into this topic.[6] It does no damage to the argument John is making nor to the overall truth of Scripture for these words not to be included in our texts.

John has made the argument (v. 4), "This is the victory that has overcome the world, even our faith." From the context, we can correctly assume that John is discussing "faith" in the incarnation, or the bodily reality, of Jesus Christ. Undoubtedly striking out at the gnostic Docetics, John further enhances his argument by stating, "Only he who believes that Jesus is the Son of God" (v. 5) truly overcomes the world.

---

[5]Earlier translations of 1 John 5:6-8 have some additional words. The KJV reads thus: "This is he that came by water and blood, even Jesus Christ; not by water only, but by water and blood. And it is the Spirit that beareth witness, because the Spirit is truth. *For there are three that bear record in heaven, the Father, the Word, and the Holy Ghost: and these three are one.* And there are three that bear witness in earth, the Spirit, and the water, and the blood: and these three agree in one." The words just quoted that are in italics were in the Latin Vulgate, but were not in any of the earlier Greek manuscripts.

[6]"Users of the *Authorized Version* [he is referring to the KJV] will be aware of a form of text which speaks first of three witnesses in heaven, and then of three witnesses on earth. The former three are the members of the Holy Trinity, the Father, the Word, and the Holy Spirit, while the latter three are the Spirit, the water, and the blood. This form of wording appears in no reputable modern version of the Bible as the actual text; most editions adopt the same practice as in the NIV of relegating the extra words to a footnote, while some (such as the RSV and NEB) totally ignore them. The words in fact occur in none of the Greek manuscripts of 1 John, except for a few late and worthless ones, and are not quoted by any early church writers. . . ." (Marshall, *The Letters of John*, pp. 235-236.)

5:6 This is the one who came by water and blood — Jesus Christ. He did not come by water only, but by water and blood.

But, who is this Jesus, the Son of God? John answers with this verse. To some readers, this is a vague passage. Marshall remarks,

> We now have a closer definition of Jesus: the person I am writing about, says John, is the One who came by water and blood, namely Jesus Christ. To the modern reader this is a statement which obscures rather than clarifies the thought. Nevertheless, it was obviously meant to draw the readers' attention to facts which would act as convincing testimony (vv. 7f.) about the person of Jesus.[7]

Cerinthus and other Gnostics would adamantly deny this, for they believed that Jesus was simply the naturally born son of Joseph and Mary. John is arguing that Jesus, on the other hand, was the divinely begotten Son of God born through a divine miracle of conception of Mary, Jesus' mother. But, what does John mean by saying that Jesus came from water and blood? Some would argue that this was referring to the physical birth, since in the mother's womb, the child is encased in water (or, amniotic fluid) and the blood involved in the birth of the child. This is not what John is arguing! In keeping with what is to follow, it seems obvious that John is discussing the water from the point of view that Jesus was baptized in water, and the blood from the point of view that Jesus shed his blood in his death. Both of these analogies would argue the physical reality of Jesus. The fact that he was baptized in water in the River Jordan seems clear enough that this was a *physical* activity. And, certainly, the shedding of blood is definitely proof that Jesus was truly human, as well as divine! It is necessary, according to John's treatment of the incarnation of God's Son, that both the water and the blood

---

[7]Ibid., p. 231.

be involved in identifying him. John's opponents undoubtedly would accept the coming by "water," while they would deny the "coming by blood."

5:7 For there are three that testify: 5:8 the Spirit, the water and the blood; and the three are in agreement.
Now, we come to the focal argument of John. Keep in mind our discussion of witnesses and the Law of Moses' requirement of two or three witnesses needed to convict one of a crime. This is evidently a very important principle that John is using to convict the Gnostic false teachers of their sin of heresy. John has been very careful to establish the fact that there are at least three witnesses for the message he is presenting. Jesus was born of a virgin, was God's Son in the flesh, had died, arisen from the dead, and had manifested himself to them. The apostle Paul had declared the certainty of the resurrection of Christ's body from the dead, for he wrote,

> For what I received I passed on to you as of first importance: that Christ died for our sins according to the Scriptures, that he was buried, that he was raised on the third day according to the Scriptures, and that he appeared to Peter, and then to the Twelve. After that, he appeared to more than five hundred of the brothers at the same time, most of whom are still living, though some have fallen asleep. Then he appeared to James, then to all the apostles, and last of all he appeared to me also, as to one abnormally born (1 Cor 15:3-8).

Whether John was personally acquainted with these words written and declared by Paul, we do not know. But, he was surely acquainted with many appearances of Jesus. What a tremendous argument the early Christians had to certify that Jesus was truly the son of man and Son of God at the same time!

But John has yet to present his most powerful argument against the Docetists: the three witnesses in verses 7 and 8. Many of the witnesses that John could call to testify would die soon; some had already died, the same with the witnesses cited by Paul. But John introduces here three *perpetual* witnesses. The three witnesses John cites now will be with us until Jesus returns to forever prove the truth of his incarnation. These three witnesses are: **the Spirit, the water, and the blood**. These three witnesses, John wrote, **are in agreement**. The Spirit refers to the Holy Spirit, whom Jesus asked his Father to send to his disciples after he had gone back to the Father (see John 14:26; 15:26; 16:5-11). From these references, we learn that the Spirit was to testify of him. He did this in many ways:

1) In their preaching,
2) In the signs and miracles the he brought them, and
3) In the inspiration which permitted the apostles to testify of him through the inspired Scriptures we have.

Every time that we read God's revelation found in the Scriptures, the Spirit is testifying that Jesus was born of the flesh and that he was fully God and fully mankind. The water, in like manner, testifies to the incarnation of Jesus. It speaks through baptism which is required of all who would believe Jesus. Every time that we see someone being baptized, that person is saying, in essence, "Watch me; my baptism testifies that I am dying to sin, that I am being buried as Jesus was, and that I am being raise from the dead." See Paul's discussion of baptism in Romans 6:1ff. The blood, which is the third witness testifies every time that a Christian eats the Lord's Supper. For, when we eat the bread and drink the cup we are saying to the world: "I am testifying to you that Jesus died and was buried for my sins, and I declare this by my partaking of the Communion." This argument by John is one of the strongest arguments I know to testify against the gnostic, docetic teaching.

5:9 We accept man's testimony, but God's testimony is greater because it is the testimony of God, which he has given about his Son.

John mildly chastises those of us who will believe what

men testify but who do not accept God's testimony. The testimony that God gives to us is stronger than any testimony mankind could give. First, *it is the testimony of God!* Should we not accept God's testimony simply because it is God's testimony? What else would we need than the assurance from God. Second, when we look at God's testimony, we have far greater evidence for its truth than we do for what mankind testifies to us. John, more than once, has given the two or three witnesses required by the Law of Moses; and then God has given us additional. Paul declared that more than five hundred had seen God's testimony. In the first chapter of 1 John, John declares that "we" have seen, heard, felt and experienced Jesus. The "we" to whom he refers is certainly more than two or three. So, we have more than ample reason to believe that God has given his Son through the incarnation to be our Savior.

5:10 Anyone who believes in the Son of God has this testimony in his heart. Anyone who does not believe God has made him out to be a liar, because he has not believed the testimony God has given about his Son.

John is giving great emphasis to the testimony of God. He mentions testimony at least eight times. And, now, he states that if one believes in God, he has this testimony in his heart. Some commentators would infer that God has given a special message into the heart of those who believe him. It is my understanding that this is not the force of his argument. I would be surprised if John would use that type of argument to the gnostic heretics since this is *their* argument: that God has given them a special knowledge. What John seems to be saying here is that it is in one's heart because believing has come from hearing, receiving, and obeying God's message. One who does not believe God is making God out to be a liar, because that person has not received nor believed in the testimony that God has provided.

5:11 And this is the testimony: God has given us eternal life, and this life is in his Son.

John now uses one of the greatest motivations for us to believe or accept God's testimony. God's testimony is greater than mankind's testimony. God's testimony is that **God has given**[8] **us eternal life.** John is not indicating that this life eternal is ours regardless of what we may do in the future. We can so sin as to lose that life, but God has already given eternal life to us. Life eternal is a "here and now" possession, not a "there and then" promise. We already possess it!

5:12 He who has the Son has life; he who does not have the Son of God does not have life.

The testimony that we have been given eternal life is based on our relation to the Son. If we accept and obey Jesus as the Son of God — both his human and divine character — then we have been given eternal life. We have already learned from our previous studies in this epistle that the gift to us is not a blind, meaningless gift. It depends on our faith, our love, and our obedience to his commands. John gave his assurance, **He who has the Son has life; he who does not have the Son of God does not have life.**

V. CONCLUDING REMARKS (5:13-21)

[13]**I write these things to you who believe in the name of the Son of God so that you may know that you have eternal life.** [14]**This is the confidence we have in approaching God: that if we ask anything according to his will, he hears us.** [15]**And if we know that he hears us — whatever we ask — we know that we have what we asked of him.**

---

[8]The Greek word for "has given" is ἔδωκεν (*edōken*, the 3rd person, singular aorist, indicative of the verb δίδωμι, "I give." The verb form indicates that God has already given to us life eternal.

¹⁶If anyone sees his brother commit a sin that does not lead to death, he should pray and God will give him life. I refer to those whose sin does not lead to death. There is a sin that leads to death. I am not saying that he should pray about that. ¹⁷All wrongdoing is sin, and there is sin that does not lead to death.

¹⁸We know that anyone born of God does not continue to sin; the one who was born of God keeps him safe, and the evil one cannot harm him. ¹⁹We know that we are children of God, and that the whole world is under the control of the evil one.

²⁰We know also that the Son of God has come and has given us understanding, so that we may know him who is true. And we are in him who is true — even in his Son Jesus Christ. He is the true God and eternal life.

²¹Dear children, keep yourselves from idols.

5:13 I write these things to you who believe in the name of the Son of God so that you may know that you have eternal life.

John begins this last section with another of his "I write these things to you . . . ." We have discussed this in other parts of this commentary. John has been very careful to let his readers know *why* he is writing to them. In John's Gospel, he was clear in showing why he wrote to them: "Jesus did many other miraculous signs in the presence of his disciples, which are not recorded in this book. But these are written that you may believe that Jesus is the Christ, the Son of God, and that by believing you may have life in his name" (John 20:30, 31). It is interesting to note how closely related are the purposes of writing the Gospel and in writing the epistle. Both are written so that we will know

1) That Jesus is the Christ, the Son of God,
2) That all can have life by believing in him and obeying his commands, and
3) To love God and our brothers.

In John's Gospel, there is ample proof of the importance of love; and in this epistle one cannot mistake the importance of love.

5:14 This is the confidence we have in approaching God: that if we ask anything according to his will, he hears us.

John reiterates the promises he has made before. If we approach God — that is, believe in him and his incarnated Son, love our brothers, and obey his commands — we will have assurance[9] or boldness to know that we do have eternal life. We are children of God, and as children, we can "ask anything according to his will, and he hears us." Jesus expressed this same idea several times during his personal ministry. In the Sermon on the Mount, Jesus said, "Ask and it will be given to you; seek and you will find; knock and the door will be opened to you. For everyone who asks receives; he who seeks finds; and to him who knocks, the door will be opened" (Matt 7:7,8). In John's Gospel, Jesus promised, "If you remain in me and my words remain in you, ask whatever you wish and it will be given (John 15:7). What a promise!

5:15 And if we know that he hears us — whatever we ask — we know that we have what we asked of him.

All too often we have failed to believe that God answers prayer. He does not give anything to us that is against his will (see Jas 4:3). For example, he does not give salvation to those who do not love him; nor does he answer the prayer of those who refuse to obey him (Heb 5:9). But, John wrote, **And if we know that he hears us — whatever we ask — we know that we have what we asked of him.** We should never ask that which is not in accordance with his plan of salvation nor what is

---

[9]The word for "assurance" is παρρησία (*parrēsia*, "courage, confidence, boldness, fearlessness"). "Confidence," the word used by the NIV, is certainly a strong word, but it seems that the word is stronger than our English word "assurance." Perhaps the use of "boldness" is a bit stronger and expresses the force of the text.

against the nature of God. But, when we do ask, we had better believe that he will answer.[10] Have you ever asked that God provide a cure for someone's illness and than been surprised when he answered you? We must leave room in our lives for trust in God's fulfillment of his promises.

sinning

5:16 If anyone sees his brother [commit a sin] that does not lead to death, he should pray and God will give him life. I refer to those whose sin does not lead to death. There is a sin that leads to death. I am not saying that he should pray about that.

This short section of 1 John is one of the most troublesome in the epistle. There are several theories that have arisen to explain the passage. However, in the light of the overall theme of the epistle, it seems to this author that only one of them satisfactorily explains it and we will consider it later. J.W. Roberts included three of these alternate interpretations, as he refers to them. They are:

> (1) that sin unto death refers to a crime for which the authorities may exact the death penalty (e.g., murder which could be a capital offense; (2) that the sin is one that the church might punish with death by asking God to visit the sinner as he did Ananias and Sapphira as recorded in Acts 5, and (3) that the sin is one which causes the church to withdraw fellowship or excommunicate the sinner. But there is no confirmation for these meanings.[11]

The troublesome expression here is "sin that leads to death" and "sin that does not lead to death," ἁμαρτία (οὐ) πρὸς θάνατον (*hamartia [ou] pros thanaton*, lit., "sin [not] toward

---

[10]The Gospels record a number of examples of asking: Matt 6:8; 7:7,11; 9:38 (for the harvest, also in Luke 10:2); 18:19 (agreement in request); 21:22; cf. Mark 10:35 (James and John ask for position in the kingdom); 11:24; Luke 11:9,13; John 11:22 (Martha petitioning on behalf of Lazarus); 14:13,14,16; 15:7,16; 16:24,26.

[11]Roberts, *The Letters of John*, p. 141.

death"). The word ἁμαρτάνοντα (*hamartanonta*, "sinning," translated "commit" in the NIV) is present tense. What do they mean? What kind of sin is he referring to? Is he saying that there are some sins that God cannot forgive? There are some other references in the New Testament that we need to address before suggesting what this writer believes John intends. Jesus warned against the "blasphemy of the Holy Spirit." "I tell you the truth, all the sins and blasphemies of men will be forgiven them. But whoever blasphemes against the Holy Spirit will never be forgiven; he is guilty of an eternal sin" (Mark 3:28, 29). "But whoever blasphemes against the Holy Spirit"[12] is a very strong warning: they shall never be forgiven! This is a very dismal warning, but Jesus infers that if one ascribes to the Holy Spirit the works of Satan, then that person has cut himself off from God and would probably never be open to accept and honor God. Another strong reference against rejecting God comes in Hebrews. That writer stated, "It is impossible for those who have once been enlightened, who have tasted the heavenly gift, who have shared in the Holy Spirit, who have tasted the goodness of the word of God and the powers of the coming age, if they fall away, to be brought back to repentance, because to their loss they are crucifying the Son of God all over again and subjecting him to public disgrace" (Heb 6:4-6). The key to this warning seems to lie in rejecting of, or crucifying of, the Son of God. If we cut off our relationship with Jesus Christ, there is nothing else, there is nobody else who can save us. This reference is parallel to Hebrews 10:26, "If we deliberately keep on sinning after we have received the knowledge of the truth, no sacrifice for sins is left." The Hebrew writer is dealing here with a

---

[12]Translated from ὃς ἂν βλασφημήσῃ εἰς τὸ πνεῦμα τὸ ἅγιον, *hos an blasphēmēsē eis to pneuma to hagion*, has the meaning of "slander, defamation, blasphemy," according to Arndt & Gingrich, pp. 142-143. In this reference it appears that Jesus is condemning those who would attribute to Jesus the role of Satan. This would be, it seems to me, a denial of the divine (Father-Son-Holy Spirit) nature of the Spirit.

different mindset of the sinner than some other references. The key to this is "deliberately keep on sinning" and "no sacrifice for sins is left." The Hebrew writer had devoted this book to those who were turning back from Christ and going back to the Law of Moses. He declares that there is no more sacrifice for sins if we reject Jesus. He is the last sacrifice; there will be no more!

John's reference to "sin unto death" (the older translations reflect the Greek construction more accurately than the NIV) seems to be a different situation. It is possible that John is using this language to indict those false teachers who were claiming that Jesus was not born in the flesh. Their sin would likely be "unto death," that is, until they died. These brothers had gone out from them. John does not name any specific sin as a "sin unto death." John does not use the article "the" in the Greek text, thus allowing the translation "sin unto death" rather than "the sin unto death." "Sin unto death" should be regarded as those sins from which no recovery is possible.

John is concerned here in this passage with a brother who commits "a sin that does not lead to death" (v. 16) which another brother sees him committing. If that sin is not "unto death" we should pray for the brother and **God will give him life** or forgiveness. John specifically states, **I refer to those whose sin does not lead to death**. He then directly refers to the **sin that does not lead to death**. He declares that **there is sin that does not lead to death**. What sin is, or whether there is a *specific sin* that leads to death, John does not tell us. But, he says, **I am not saying that he should pray about that**. This statement is difficult for us to interpret. There is definitely sin that leads to death and sin that does not lead to death. What that specific sin is, John does not say. However, undoubtedly those who were reading John's original letter surely would have known. This is the reason this writer associates the "sin unto death" as the rejection of the humanity of Jesus; hence, he seems to be directing his teaching to the gnostic Docetics about whom this entire letter is concerned.

5:17 All wrongdoing is sin, and there is sin that does not lead to death.

John sets about now to tell us what sin is. **Wrongdoing**, from αδικια,[13] which has the meaning of "unright living." He intensifies the meaning of this statement by stating that "all wrongdoing, or unrighteousness, is sin." Furthermore, he states that there is some wrongdoing **that does not lead to death.** (See previous discussion for more about "sin unto death."

5:18 We know that anyone born of God does not continue to sin; the one who was born of God keeps him safe, and the evil one cannot harm him.

We have already seen that the one born of God does not live a life of sin (see comments on 1 John 3:6 and 9). Here, John adds another dimension to this concept. He says, **the one who was born of God keeps him safe.** This statement is a little ambivalent on first reading. He is not talking about "anyone born of God," but the "one born of God" undoubtedly referring to Jesus. He is the center of all of John's argument. The Docetics were dividing the church and spreading the heresy that Jesus was not God's Son, born of the virgin Mary. John says, this is the one who keeps the ones born of God safe. Jesus has conquered death, the last stronghold of Satan, and Satan cannot touch God's children. Believing that Jesus is the Son of God in the flesh, obeying his commands and loving the brothers is a shield against Satan.

5:19 We know that we are children of God, and that the whole world is under the control of the evil one. 5:20 We know also that the Son of God has come and has given us understanding, so that we may know him who is true. And we are in him who is true — even in his Son Jesus Christ. He

---

[13]Ἀδικία, the opposite of δικαιοσύνη, *dikaiosynē*, "uprightness, righteousness, carries the concept of righteousness." elsewhere, sin is referred to as "lawlessness" and in other places it is "missing the mark."

is the true God and eternal life.

In his concluding remarks, John hits repeatedly on the theme that the Christian has knowledge that is directly contradictory to the mystical knowledge the Gnostic claimed. Christ brought to us both understanding of God's nature, and eternal life, because he not only came from God, but is the true God.

5:21 Dear children, keep yourselves from idols.

The final exhortation by John, to keep away from idols, stands in for all that he has said earlier in the letter about walking in the light and not continuing to sin. Whether the particular form of this final instruction indicates a Gentile audience or not, idol worship was a problem that had plagued God's people throughout the history of the world. In the early days of the Ephesian church, before they "lost [their] first love" (Rev 2:4), the Ephesian Christians had been very conscientious in cutting themselves off from their old practices — so much so that it affected the city's economy as recorded in Acts 19. John's concern is that his "dear children" be just as conscientious that nothing take the place of the true God, revealed to us in the Word made Flesh (John 1:14).

THE BOOK OF
2 JOHN

OUTLINE

2 JOHN

[1]The elder, To the chosen lady and her children, whom I love in the truth — and not I only, but also all who know the truth — [2]because of the truth, which lives in us and will be with us forever:

[3]Grace, mercy and peace from God the Father and from Jesus Christ, the Father's Son, will be with us in truth and love. [4]It has given me great joy to find some of your children walking in the truth, just as the Father commanded us. [5]And now, dear lady, I am not writing you a new command but one we have had from the beginning. I ask that we love one another. [6]And this is love: that we walk in obedience to his commands. As you have heard from the beginning, his command is that you walk in love.

[7]Many deceivers, who do not acknowledge Jesus Christ as coming in the flesh, have gone out into the world. Any such person is the deceiver and the antichrist. [8]Watch out that you do not lose what you have worked for, but that you may be rewarded fully. [9]Anyone who runs ahead and does not continue in the teaching of Christ does not have God; whoever continues in the teaching has both the Father and the Son. [10]If anyone comes to you and does not bring this teaching, do not take him into your house or welcome him. [11]Anyone who welcomes him shares in his wicked work.

[12]I have much to write to you, but I do not want to use paper and ink. Instead, I hope to visit you and talk with you face to face, so that our joy may be complete.

[13]The children of your chosen sister send their greetings.

I. GREETING (1-3)

As was mentioned earlier, 2 and 3 John are closer examples of first century letters than 1 John. We have author, recipient, greeting, transitional statement of thanks or praise, main body, and closing. John continues to answer the same villains in his second epistle as he had in the first. This is not to say that there were Gnostics under every rock opposing the church in the first century, but rather that John specifically answers their false teaching with his epistles.

Aside from inspiration and God's canonization of the works, their preservation indicates the respect given to John's writings by the church. The readers needed to hear that they were wanted by God, that they were chosen by him, that they were protected by him from various enemy threats.

v. 1 The elder,[1]

The letter writer is πρεσβύτερος (*presbyteros*). Taken literally, this word means "older one." It was used for:

1) Those of an older or advanced age

2) Those in church leadership (usually used in plurality in the NT; see 1 Pet 5:1)

3) Predecessors, people of ancient times. One possibility is that John is using apocalyptic language to disguise himself and to protect the readers from government persecution. In any case, John is known by the readers of this letter and simply uses the designation of **The Elder.**

To the chosen lady and her children,

The recipients of the letter is another matter for discussion. Commentators through the centuries have disagreed about their identification. Who are **the chosen lady and her children?** There are at least four views to consider for the identification of the lady:

---

[1]See discussion by G.M. Burge, "John, Letters of," *DLNT,* p. 595.

COLLEGE PRESS NIV COMMENTARY

1) Some have argued that the **lady** is an "unknown sister" in one of the local congregations. This is probably the best position for those who insist on the one-recipient view.

2) Others have held that there was a lady by the name of Eklecte or Eclecta (literally taking the Greek to indicate an actual name of a specific woman, Ἐκλεκτῇ, (transliterated as *Eklecte*). E.g., Clement of Alexandria held this view. It is also less likely because we find it again as an adjective in verse 13.

3) Perhaps it was another lady named Kuria or Cyria by transliterating the word for lady (κυρία in Greek, the equivalent of "Martha" in Hebrew). But there is little evidence in early Christian literature to support such a view.

4) If John were using the device of cryptic language in this epistle, **the chosen lady and her children** would be the local church.

It is my opinion that this last view is the correct one.[2] Both the Greek pronouns and verb forms used here are plural. The **children**, therefore, would be members of a local congregation (see 1 Tim 1:2; Gal 4:25). Like mother, like daughter — the church and her members are chosen!

whom I love in the truth — and not I only, but also all who know the truth —

John and the recipients share a common passion for the truth. He is referring to the *gospel* of truth (John 1: 7; 14:7; 17:19; Gal 2:5, 14; Col 1:6). John identifies himself as being a

---

[2]Among those who hold this view: William Barclay, *The Letters of John* (Philadelphia: Westminster, 1976), p. 138; I.H. Marshall, *The Epistles of John*, The New International Commentary on the New Testament (Grand Rapids: Eerdmans, 1979), p. 60; A.E. Brooke, *A Critical and Exegetical Commentary on the Johannine Epistles*, International Critical Commentary (Edinburgh: T. & T. Clark, 1971), p. lxxxl; Edward A. McDowell, *Hebrews-Revelation*, The Broadman Bible Commentary, Vol. 12 (Nashville: Broadman) p. 226; J.W. Roberts, *The Letters of John*, p. 150; Brooke Foss Westcott (guardedly), *The Epistles of St. John: The Greek Text with Notes and Essays* (London: Macmillan, 1883), p. 214; and Stott, *The Epistles of John*, pp. 200-201.

part of their company. **All who** have obeyed the gospel **know the truth** and are known by the truth they live. Paul bragged about congregations whose reputation in the faith preceded them (Rom 1:8; 2 Cor 8:7; Ph 1:15; Col 1:4; 1 Thess 1:8; and 2 Thess 1:3).

v. 2 because of the truth,

Truth (ἀλήθεια,[3] *alētheia*) is a key word in the second epistle appearing five times in the first four verses. Notice the antithesis of truth in the word "deceivers" in verse 7 and the intimated opposition to truth in verse 11, "wicked work." For the sake of the truth John is writing to these Christians to remind them of a common cause and bloodline.

which lives in us and will be with us forever:

How does this *truth* live[4] in the Christian? *Jesus* is the truth (John 14:6). When we clothe ourselves with Christ, we clothe ourselves with him, the truth (Gal 3:26-29). Jesus' promise in Matthew 28:20 is fulfilled by the indwelling of Christ's Spirit (John 14:16; Acts 2:38, 39) and our continued faithfulness to his revealed truth in the Word.

v. 3 Grace, mercy and peace

These three words also appear in 1 Timothy 1:2 and 2 Timothy 1:2. You have the common Greek greeting in **grace** (χάρις, *charis*) and the common Hebrew greeting in **peace** (εἰρήνη, *eirēnē* — often explained as the Christian form

---

[3]See Marshall, *The Epistles of John*, n. 15, p. 62; see also M.J. Wilkins' discussion of the key words "truth and love" in John's epistles, "Pastoral Theology," *DLNT*, pp. 880-881.

[4]The Greek verb (μένω) translated in older versions as "abides" is used 41 times in John's Gospel; 26 times in the Epistles, and only once in Revelation. John used the word more than all the other NT writers combined. (J. B. Smith, *Greek-English Concordance to the New Testament* [Scottdale, PA: Herald Press, 1955], p. 226.)

of *shalom*). **Mercy** (ἔλεος, *eleos*) serves as the bridge connecting the two (Westcott, "the manifestation of the divine 'grace.'"[5]).

from God the Father and from Jesus Christ, the Father's Son, will be with us in truth and love.

John presents evidence that **Jesus Christ**[6] and **God the Father** are one in that they are the source (παρὰ, *para* or from) of the grace, mercy and peace. Literally these blessings come from both equally. Jesus had told Philip, "Anyone who has seen me has seen the Father" (John 14:9). John is also answering some of the false teaching that denied Jesus' physical birth and life on earth (v. 7). Grace, mercy and peace will cohabit with the Christian through **truth and love**.[7] Interestingly, here the verb tense is future ἔσται (2 Pet 1:2 and Jude 2 use present tense, "be. . .in abundance" — πληθύνω, *plēthynō*).

II. WALKING IN OBEDIENCE (4-6)

A. SOURCE OF JOY (4)

v. 4 It has given me great joy to find some of your children walking in the truth, just as the Father commanded us.

Following the customary first century letter form, John expresses a note of thanksgiving to the recipients. As for any parent, the knowledge that your children are actually obedient to what you have asked them to do is a source of **great joy**, not to mention relief! God the Father has commanded that we continue to walk **in the truth**. Logically if **some** (not

---

[5]Westcott, *The Epistles of St. John*, p. 215.

[6]"Lord" is added by the Textus Receptus — see Bruce M. Metzger, *A Textual Commentary on the Greek New Testament*, [Third Edition], (New York: United Bible Societies, 1971), p. 721.

[7]Brooke, *The Johannine Epistles*, p.171 — "The two vital elements of the Christian Faith, the possession of the highest knowledge and its expression in action. They are the keynotes of the Epistle."

in the original[8]) of the children were **walking in the truth**, others were no longer and had fallen away. It is to be a lifestyle for the faithful that is obvious to everyone, friend and enemy alike.

B. LOVE AS OBEDIENCE (5-6)

v. 5 And now, dear lady, I am not writing you a new command but one we have had from the beginning. I ask that we love one another.

The apostle of love again politely pleads with his readers (singular, yet addressed to all, including John) to obey the **command**[9] to **love one another**. The NIV uses the words **I ask**. It is *not new* because they have heard it before. John had seen, touched and heard it before. The command goes back to Leviticus 19:18. More specifically, **from the beginning** would be from the time of their rebirth and being clothed with truth and love (John 13:34; see comments on 1 John 2:7-15). In contrast, the Gnostics were constantly adding new teachings. The old teaching of love was sufficient to answer the new threat to the church. It is not optional because it is a command from the head of the church. Jesus in Matthew 22 and Paul in Romans 13 summed up a list of commands in the one to love.

v. 6 And this is love: that we walk in obedience to his commands. As you have heard from the beginning, his command is that you walk in love.

John defines love for the readers again. We have the benefit of knowing what John has written in his extant writings.

---

[8]Although not in the Greek, the context requires it. Since John speaks of "great joy," it is presumed that the majority of the church is faithful. (Roberts, *The Letters of John*, p. 156).

[9]Alexander Ross suggests that this is proof that 1 and 2 John had the same author, *Commentary on the Epistles of James and John* New International Commentary (Grand Rapids: Eerdmans, 1970), p. 229.

They did not and needed another explanation of love fleshed out. The same phrase is repeated, **from the beginning**. John reinforces the thought that they knew better and should renew their first love.

But what happens when we do not obey *all* of **his commands?** We have "one who speaks to the Father in our defense — Jesus Christ, the Righteous One" (1 John 2:1). Intent to obey his commands and living a life before and toward God proves our love for him and our neighbor. Maybe the RSV has a closer meaning to the original by using "follow" in love. Jesus best demonstrated how to love and we must follow his example! Walking in love puts our confession of faith into action.

III. CONTINUING IN THE TEACHING (7-11)

A. IDENTIFICATION OF DECEIVERS (7)

v. 7 Many deceivers, who do not acknowledge Jesus Christ as coming in the flesh, have gone out into the world. Any such person is the deceiver and the antichrist.

This is the real reason for John to write about the truth — the rise of false teachers. The NIV does not translate ὅτι (*hoti* — "because" or "for") at the beginning of the verse, which would evidence John's purpose in warning. We generally know what deceivers are. They are liars! And we know that the devil "is a liar and the father of lies" (John 8:44). They had been commissioned by their master to go **out into the world**. John clarifies that the deceivers attempting to teach among his readers would be those who deny Jesus' incarnation (see 1 John 2:22; 4:2, 15; 5:6). They **do not acknowledge** or confess (ὁμολογέω, *homologeō*) that Jesus came in the flesh in contrast to the Christian confession. Their unity is in a common conspiracy of deceit. They are calling God a liar (1 John 5:10).

145

One of the best safeguards against error or false teaching is for brothers and sisters to genuinely love one another.[10]

The definite article appears in the original to label false teachers as **the deceiver and the antichrist.** Some have taken this to mean that the false teachers were the devil himself. There is no worse enemy for Christians than one who is anti-Christ. In this wording we hear the strongest warning from John. That is why any association with the deceivers would be anti-Christian and walking in the opposite direction of their confession of faith and walk in love. Is there *one* Antichrist? John is the only New Testament writer to use the terminology, here and in 1 John 2:18, 22 and 4:3. Context indicates that there are many antichrists or deceivers.

B. BEING FULLY REWARDED (8)

v. 8 Watch out that you do not lose what you have worked for, but that you may be rewarded fully.

Watch out (βλέπετε, *blepete*) means caution! When one holds the belief that Jesus did not come in the flesh, as Knofel Staton responds, "it is just a logical jump to conclude that He is not presently coming into the flesh of men via the Holy Spirit. If that is denied, ethics is reduced to humanism. That is precisely what Gnosticism did to ethics in the first century. If there is no Divine that comes into the human, the human becomes his own god."[11] If a person becomes "his own god," he is lost.

John's warning here runs counter to the position of some Calvinists who hold the doctrine of "the perseverance of the saints" (the "P" in TULIP[12]). The possibility of losing, drifting

[10]Westcott, *The Epistles of John*, p. 218.

[11]Knofel Staton, *Thirteen Lessons on First, Second, and Third John* (Joplin: College Press, 1980), p. 131.

[12]The word TULIP is used as an acronym for the Calvinistic doctrine of Total Depravity, Unconditional Election, Limited Atonement, Irresistible Grace; and Perseverance of the Saints.

away or falling away is taught in such passages as Hebrews 2:1 (drifting), Matthew 11:6; 26:31, 33; Mark 4:17; 14:27, 29; Luke 7:23; 8:13; and Hebrews 6:6 (falling). The NIV translates the clause, ἅ ἠργασάμεθα (*ha ērgasametha*) as **what you have worked for**. This is better rendered, "what *we* have worked for." The objection to works salvation would be answered to some degree with this interpretation. We would see John's concern that his own efforts and those of other evangelists could be in vain should the readers "fall away." Paul writes, "continue to work out your salvation with fear and trembling, for it is God who works in you to will and to act according to his good purpose" (Phil 2:12, 13).

There is always a need for self-examination in the Christian life (e.g., 1 Cor 11:28). The end result of our watching out is to **be rewarded fully**. "Reward" is used 24 times in the New Testament, among which only one other passage is in John's writings, Revelation 22:12. The ultimate reward for the Christian to hear from his Lord is, "Well done, good and faithful servant! You have been faithful with a few things; I will put you in charge of many things. Come and share your master's happiness!" (Matt 25: 21).

C. HAVING BOTH THE FATHER AND THE SON (9)

v. 9 Anyone who runs ahead and does not continue in the teaching of Christ does not have God;
What does John mean by the clause **anyone who runs ahead,** as the NIV translates Πᾶς ὁ προάγων (*pas ho proagōn*)? It can also mean "to go too far" or as Smith uses the alternate reading of παραβαίνων, *parabainōn*[13] – "progresses," which can also mean "turn away" or "leave." There is a caution for John's readers, as well as for us, to build on the past without

---

[13]David Smith, *The Epistles of John*, The Expositor's Greek Testament, Vol. V (Grand Rapids: Eerdmans, n.d.), p. 202.

completely abandoning it. John describes a person who is not satisfied with the way things are and usurps a teacher's authority in order to present a contradictory new teaching. He or she has a revelation that is better than what God has revealed. When that happens, he stops following **the teaching of Christ** and **does not have God!** To be without Christ is to be lost (1 John 5:12).

What then is the teaching of Christ? Two options would be either "*what* Jesus taught" or "what has been taught *about* him." The context of John's epistles would have us adopt the latter view due to the false teaching about the Christ of which John warns his readers.

whoever continues in the teaching has both the Father and the Son.

The positive outcome for the faithful follower is the assurance of having **both the Father and the Son** and their having him. Persevering of the saints requires discipline!

D. WARNING ABOUT MISDIRECTED HOSPITALITY (10-11)

v. 10 If anyone comes to you and does not bring this teaching, do not take him into your house or welcome him.

If begins a conditional sentence and means in essence that it is likely that the recipients of this letter *will* encounter false teachers. Marshall comments, "we should not give any kind of practical encouragement to the false teachers."[14] We have heard that some cults practice scare tactics in warning their would-be proselytes to ignore any other teaching as from the devil. That would be one way for false teachers to protect their catch. John warns the Christians to identify the deceivers immediately by their speech. If what they teach is not in line with what John has described as the teaching of Christ (or the teaching about

---

[14]Marshall, *The Epistles of John*, p. 74.

Christ), they are to be avoided entirely. Romans 12:13 is not to be applied to false teachers and deceivers. Christians are under no obligation to "practice hospitality" to them. **Do not take him into your house or welcome him** clearly protects family devotion to one another and to Christ.[15]

Ross cautions about overreacting and becoming too judgmental, "We should, however, be absolutely certain that men are as far astray from Christian Truth as John's heretics were before we think of meeting [sic] out to them such treatment as John here recommends."[16] We would all do well to apply 1 John 4:1-6 in testing the spirits of such alleged teachers in order to protect ourselves and the fellowship of the church.

v. 11 Anyone who welcomes him shares in his wicked work.

If the readers had not learned the lesson by now, John adds to the warning by explaining that to be hospitable to deceivers is the same as being a deceiver. They would have fellowship (κοινωνία, *koinōnia*) in wickedness! Alexander Campbell used the phrase "listening distance" or "hearing distance." Ross comments that inviting deceivers in, "would increase their opportunities for working mischief."[17] Paul warned, "I urge you brothers . . . . Keep away from them." (Rom 16:17). If we do not invite false teachers into our homes (churches — Acts 2:46; 1 Cor 16:19; Phlm 2), we will not come within the listening distance to be led astray!

IV. HOPING FOR A VISIT (12)

v. 12 I have much to write to you, but I do not want to use paper and ink.

A close parallel with 3 John indicates that both books may

---

[15]Westcott, *The Epistles of John*, p. 220. "Whatever may be thought of the application the picture of family devotion is of singular interest."

[16]Ross, *Commentary on the Epistles of James and John*, p. 232.

[17]Ibid., p. 231.

have been written at the same time. We do not know how **much** more John wished **to write** to the readers of this letter. The brevity[18] of the letter demonstrates John's urgency in warning the church. Many have speculated concerning what John might have written. It is reminiscent of John 21:25 where John ends his portrait of Jesus and claims that many more volumes would still not contain all of his life. If John has been using a disguise throughout the letter through cryptic language, he may have been protecting his readers from detection by not saying too much in writing.

Instead, I hope to visit you and talk with you face to face, so that our joy may be complete.

He would wait to speak with them **face to face.** Some things you cannot write in a letter, speak over the phone or by electronic mail. He may have planned to equip them more completely to handle the onslaught of the false teachers and to rejoice with them in their common faith. Again, John includes himself by using the word **our** and remains consistent with the rest of the letter. John wanted to rejoice with them and in person.

V. CLOSING (13)

v. 13 The children of your chosen sister send their greetings.

John closes his letter as he began it. If John has been addressing a local congregation, he then signs his letter by sending reciprocal greetings from his own congregation. They needed to know that they were not alone in the world. If John is writing from Ephesus, it is the church at Ephesus

---

[18]F.F. Bruce, *The Epistles of John* (Old Tappan, NJ: Revell, 1970), p. 143 — brevity of the letter was practical in order to fit all of the writing on one sheet of papyrus.

that sends greetings. The Textus Receptus has ἀμήν (*amēn*) added to the closing words of the verse, **your chosen sister** (literally: your sister, the chosen one).

THE BOOK OF
3 JOHN

OUTLINE

3 JOHN

[1]The elder, To my dear friend Gaius, whom I love in the truth.

[2]Dear friend, I pray that you may enjoy good health and that all may go well with you, even as your soul is getting along well. [3]It gave me great joy to have some brothers come and tell about your faithfulness to the truth and how you continue to walk in the truth. [4]I have no greater joy than to hear that my children are walking in the truth.

[5]Dear friend, you are faithful in what you are doing for the brothers, even though they are strangers to you. [6]They have told the church about your love. You will do well to send them on their way in a manner worthy of God. [7]It was for the sake of the Name that they went out, receiving no help from the pagans. [8]We ought therefore to show hospitality to such men so that we may work together for the truth.

[9]I wrote to the church, but Diotrephes, who loves to be first, will have nothing to do with us. [10]So if I come, I will call attention to what he is doing, gossiping maliciously about us. Not satisfied with that, he refuses to welcome the brothers. He also stops those who want to do so and puts them out of the church.

[11]Dear friend, do not imitate what is evil but what is good. Anyone who does what is good is from God. Anyone who does what is evil has not seen God. [12]Demetrius is well spoken of by everyone⁻and even by the truth itself. We also speak well of him, and you know that our testimony is true.

¹³I have much to write you, but I do not want to do so
with pen and ink.
¹⁴I hope to see you soon, and we will talk face to face.
Peace to you. The friends here send their greetings.
Greet the friends there by name.

I. GREETING (1)

The shortest book in the New Testament is a very special,
personal letter. Four major characters play roles in the book:
John, Gaius, Diotrephes, and Demetrius. Although the names
of "Jesus" and "Christ" do not appear in 3 John, the "Name"
in verse 7 likely stands in substitution for the Lord Jesus.

v. 1 The elder,

One of the evidences that John did indeed write 3 John is
the use of the same address as in 2 John 1, the elder (see earlier comments). The brevity of both 2 and 3 John argue for
the possibility that the material only warranted the use of
one papyrus sheet. He was being practical yet succinct with
his messages.

To my dear friend Gaius, whom I love in the truth.
Friend is used four times in this letter (9 times in John's
writings). It translates ἀγαπητός (*agapētos*) in which we can see
the word for love (*agapē*) and why some versions use
"beloved." The NIV has chosen to interpret John's sentiment
with the word **dear**.

Who is Gaius? The name was as common as John's in New
Testament times. The Gaius addressed here should not be
confused with others by the same name in Acts 19:29 (the riot
at Ephesus); 20:4 (the collection for Jerusalem saints);
Romans 16:23 (housed Paul in Corinth); or 1 Corinthians
1:14 (perhaps the same as the one in Romans whom Paul had

immersed into Christ). It would be speculative to identify Gaius as anyone other than a prominent leader in the church who received a personal letter from his friend John.

II. GAIUS ADMONISHED (2-8)

A. WALKING IN THE TRUTH (2-4)

v. 2 Dear friend, I pray that you may enjoy good health and that all may go well with you, even as your soul is getting along well.

John demonstrates his concern for both the physical and spiritual health[1] of Gaius by praying personally for his total wellbeing. This is not a prooftext for the health-wealth gospel. As J.W. Roberts points out, "In Timothy the verb [ὑγιαίνειν, *hygiainein*] used here (be in health) always has a figurative sense of doctrine that is 'healthy' or 'sound'."[2]

v. 3 It gave me great joy to have some brothers come and tell about your faithfulness to the truth and how you continue to walk in the truth.

In a similar manner as Paul discovered news from the churches (1 Cor 1:11; Phil 4:18), John has heard from other brothers regarding Gaius. Again, the NIV does not translate γὰρ (*gar*, for)[3] as a purposeful transition into verse 3. John has the same type of joy for Gaius as he had in 2 John for those who would remain faithful.

---

[1]William Barclay says, "John was like Jesus; he never forgot that men have bodies as well as souls and that they matter, too" (*The Letters of John*, p. 148).

[2]J.W.Roberts, *The Letters of John*, p. 172.

[3]According to Metzger, the NIV committee had reason not to consider the word as part of the original text. However, "the word γαρ is adequately supported by a variety of witnesses . . . ." (*Textual Commentary*, p. 723).

v. 4 I have no greater joy than to hear that my children are walking in the truth.

One would not expect to read of such *great* **joy**[4] knowing what John writes about Diotrephes later in the same letter. He had heard about the faith of his **children** because they were **walking in the truth.** They were putting John's teaching into practice despite any of Satan's attacks. They had gone beyond hearing the truth to actually living it. "It was from truth, believed and obeyed by his children, that he derived his greatest joy."[5] As James 1:24 teaches, "You see that a person is justified by what he does and not by faith alone." We would do well to learn the lesson that the need to nurture new Christians on to maturity is as important as bringing them to spiritual birth.

B. FAITHFUL IN WORKING TOGETHER (5-8)

1. Faithful Actions with Brothers (5-6)

v. 5 Dear friend, you are faithful in what you are doing for the brothers, even though they are strangers to you.

John praises his **friend** for having practiced the kind of hospitality to strangers described in Hebrews 13:2. It was meeting a need for unknown individuals who may never have a way to repay the favor. Some have commented that 3 John is not centered on "doctrine." Yet a proper understanding of the doctrine of Christian hospitality[6] is vital to the life of the church! These brothers were likely traveling missionaries who preached the gospel. (These strangers might have informed

---

[4]There is some discussion as to whether the original word here is χάριν (grace) or χαράν (joy). Most agree that the latter is the preferred reading. This is an intriguing possibility if the alternate is John's original thought.

[5]J.R.W. Stott, *The Epistles of John*, p. 220.

[6]See the discussion of hospitality in Barclay, *The Letters of John*, pp. 148-151; see also D.F. Watson, "Rhetoric, Rhetorical Criticism," *DLNT*, p. 1047 — 3 John is concerned with "the nature and necessity of hospitality."

John of Gaius' faith.) Jesus experienced hospitality on several occasions. Jesus also taught his disciples what to expect in their travels. Matthew 10:10 teaches that a true and genuine "worker is worthy of his keep." Just as those who are hospitable to false teachers share in their wickedness, so those who take care of Christian family members share in the truth.

v. 6 They have told the church about your love.
By Gaius' act of hospitality, he expressed the **love** of Christ. The strangers publicly acknowledged to their own congregation the love and care given to them. This is the only instance where John uses the term for **church** (ἐκκλησία, *ekklēsia* or "called out ones," see vv. 9 and 10). The act of giving can cause others to give. Paul provokes the Corinthians to give as the Macedonian churches had done sacrificially (2 Cor 8:1-7). We could learn to urge one another to love and good deeds (Heb 10:24).

You will do well to send them on their way in a manner worthy of God.
F.F. Bruce claims that the expression "you will do well" is idiomatic for either making a polite request "or expressing thanks in advance."[7] One of the ways we can hear the "well done" from the Master is to support those who propagate the gospel. We will be doing what pleases God. **In a manner worthy of God** can mean "as if you were sending God himself on the journey"(see Matt 10:40). Christ's body has many members with many gifts. Some can serve as missionaries and others are "called out" to support the evangelists.

2. Proper Hospitality (7-8)

v. 7 It was for the sake of the Name that they went out, receiving no help from the pagans.

---

[7]F.F. Bruce, *The Epistles of John*, p. 150.

John explains why the strangers had gone out. **They went out** for Jesus' sake, in his **Name**. The apostles had been warned by the Sanhedrin in Jerusalem not to preach "in the name of Jesus" (Acts 5:40). The same verb is used for the false teachers as "they went out." The obvious difference is motive: one group went out in the name of the devil, the other, in the Name of the Creator and Lord of the Universe! The missionaries had gone out without the **help from the pagans**. It appears that one congregation or group of congregations had supported the missionaries so that they need not charge the pagans (or anyone else) for preaching.

v. 8 We ought therefore to show hospitality to such men so that we may work together for the truth.

These are the ones to welcome. Avoid false teachers who deny that Jesus came in the flesh, but **show hospitality** to the Lord's laborers! We **ought** to do so in order that or with the result that we will **work together for the truth**. Such giving comes out of gratitude and not out of a legalistic obligation. The Lord's work is mutually benefited by our selflessness. Moffatt reads, "allies for the Truth."

III. DIOTREPHES CONDEMNED (9-10)

v. 9 I wrote to the church, but Diotrephes, who loves to be first, will have nothing to do with us.

While Gaius is a good example, **Diotrephes** is a bad example for church leadership. I wonder what John had written **to the church** that caused him to **have nothing to do with** him? Diotrephes exhibits an arrogance that enthroned himself as a "ruling elder" or at least a self-proclaimed leader. We do not know what position or function Diotrephes held in the local congregation. He may have been a teacher, an evangelist, or other leader. The missing letter from John to the church may have revealed who he was and what he did.

Who loves to be first is analyzed by Westcott to mean that ambition was his main fault and not necessarily any other false teaching.[8] (The following verse shows what an evil root of self-love can produce.) He loved the wrong person first. Besides, Diotrephes had the audacity to reject an apostle of the Lord! John had learned from the Master himself, that to be first you have to be willing to be last. The greatest is the servant. We do not know if Diotrephes is later salvageable through additional efforts by John himself or others. We can speculate that since we have no other written confirmation to the contrary, Diotrephes' story ends in this letter.

v. 10 So if I come, I will call attention to what he is doing, gossiping maliciously about us.
Will Diotrephes continue to have nothing to do with John once they meet face to face? Gaius is reading an advanced warning that probably reached Diotrephes. It would have caught the attention of most people and prompted repentance.
Romans 1:29 and 1 Timothy 5:13 speak of "gossips." The classic definition of gossip has been the sharing of information about someone else when you are neither part of the problem nor part of the solution. The malicious **gossiping** described by John raises out of envy for apostolic authority and brazen defiance of the Lord. It is the type of tongue set on fire by hell itself (Jas 3:6). Literally, his "nonsense" will expose him for who he really is and Gaius need not concern himself with a direct challenge of Diotrephes.

Not satisfied with that, he refuses to welcome the brothers.
The undermining tactic used by Diotrephes is compounded with his blatant refusal **to welcome the brothers.** He has hospitality reversed. The ones he should welcome, he refuses. One can conclude that he welcomes the likes of false teachers with

---

[8]B.F. Westcott, *The Epistles of John*, p. 229.

whom he shares common motives. He shares in their wicked deeds and finds fellowship (*koinōnia*) with the deceivers.

He also stops those who want to do so and puts them out of the church.

As if refusing the brothers was not enough, Diotrephes keeps others from giving and excommunicates them! Envy is evidenced by his actions. This fleshly emotion operates from the philosophy "if I cannot have something, I will see that no one else can either." The Lord did not appoint this man to leadership in the church. He had no authority to put anyone out of the church (perhaps applying Paul's example in 1 Cor 5:5, but apart from divine revelation or inspiration). He is doing the exact opposite of what John has encouraged Gaius to do. Second John 9 applied to Diotrephes would categorize him along with the gentiles who are without hope and "without God in the world" (Eph 2:12). Jesus prophesied that we would know people by their fruit, good or bad (Matt 7:16, 20) — this leads us into the next verse.

IV. DEMETRIUS COMMENDED (11-12)

v. 11 Dear friend, do not imitate what is evil but what is good.

Gaius is addressed personally to regain his attention for instruction. John has described **what is evil**, now he will define **what is good**. Do not mimic (μὴ μιμοῦ, *mē mimou* — **do not imitate**) the evil, but *do* imitate the good. The apostle may not have intended to limit the example of evil to Diotrephes and the good to Demetrius.[9] The reader naturally draws that

---

[9]A.E. Brooke, *A Critical and Exegetical Commentary on the Johannine Epistles*, p. 191 — sums up the verse, "Viewed rightly, it is simply a matter of refusing the evil and choosing the good."

conclusion from the context simply because the contrasts are immediately obvious.

Anyone who does what is good is from God.
The lifestyle of doing **good** or right is **from God** (or of God: 1 John 3:10; 4:4, 6; 5:19). **Anyone** doing good (ὁ ἀγαθοποιῶν, *ho agathopoiōn*) means a life full of the Holy Spirit (Acts 6:3) and recognizable by the fruit (Gal 5:22, 23). If you want to know how to discern a person's motives, observe his or her fruit.

Anyone who does what is evil has not seen God.
John 14:9, "Anyone who has seen me has seen the Father" and 1 John 3:6, "No one who continues to sin has either seen him or known him." **Anyone who does what is evil** is outside of the fellowship. Evil-doers are experiencing the effects of "excommunication" without being excommunicated! Neither will they see God in the future should they continue to sin without repentance and restoration.

v. 12 Demetrius is well spoken of by everyone ⁻ and even by the truth itself. We also speak well of him,
Who is Demetrius? Some have speculated that he was Demas named in Colossians 4:14; Philemon 24 and 2 Timothy 4:10.[10] Although it is not defensible to identify this Demetrius with the one in Acts 19:24, Luke records the incident (in Ephesus) of a Demetrius who opposed Paul. Could the Demetrius in Acts 19 have become a Christian by the time John wrote 3 John? Since the name is as common perhaps as either John or Gaius, this Demetrius probably is a unique individual possibly a leader among the missionaries. Roberts suggests that he may have been the courier for this letter.[11]

---

[10]E.g., J.R.W. Stott, *The Epistles of John*, p. 229 and Brooke, *The Johannine Epistles*, p.192.

[11]J.W. Roberts, *The Letters of John*, p. 180. As also Brooke, *The Johannine Epistles*, p. 192; B. F. Westcott, *The Epistles of John*, p. 231, et al.

John used three witnesses in 1 John 5:7-8 and repeats the pattern here by giving testimony to the character of Demetrius. He is:

1) **Well spoken by everyone** — possibly by Christians and outsiders alike
2) **Even by the truth itself** — by the facts or by the Lord himself (John 14:6)
3) **We speak well of him** — John and those in Ephesus who knew him.

and you know that our testimony is true.

The last part of verse 12 should be associated directly with the testimony of John and those with him. They knew John personally and could take his word and that of the sister church for Demetrius.

V. DESIRE TO SPEAK IN PERSON (13-14)

v. 13 I have much to write you, but I do not want to do so with pen and ink.

Verse 13 parallels 2 John 12. There is only a slight variation, with the one letter being directed to a congregation, the latter, to an individual. Here John uses **pen and ink** — μέλανος καὶ καλάμου (*melanos kai kalamou*) while he uses "paper and ink" — χάρτου καὶ μέλανος (*chartou kai melanos*). This similarity between the epistles argues for John's authorship. He could have written much more than would fit onto one sheet of papyrus! His not wanting to write is not a sign of laziness but rather a testament to his personal concern to communicate in person.

v. 14 I hope to see you soon, and we will talk face to face.

John's **hope** is to actually **see** Gaius **face to face** (literally mouth to mouth — στόμα πρὸς στόμα, *stoma pros stoma*). **Soon** (εὐθέως, *eutheōs*) is elsewhere translated "immediately" 32 times

in the New Testament (80 times all together with similar con-
notations). If the crisis caused by Diotrephes is as critical as
indicated above, a personal visit is warranted very soon to set
things in order.

**Peace to you. The friends here send their greetings. Greet
the friends there by name.**
Shalom! The common Hebrew greeting had been adopted
by many early Christians since many of the first converts
came directly out of Judaism. **Peace** (εἰρήνη, *eirēnē*) was
promised to his followers by Jesus. (See John 14:27; 16:33;
20:19, 21, 26; 1 Pet 5:14.) Diotrephes had been offering the
opposite to the church. Christians experience a mutual peace
with God (Rom 5:1) and are commanded to "make every
effort to do what leads to peace and to mutual edification"
(Rom 14:19).
The friends here are from John's congregation (especially
if 2 and 3 John were written at the same time). It speaks well
of their fellowship and common cause to be named as friends,
a tie that indeed binds Christians together. Individuals are
important to John and to God (John 10:3; Rev 3:5; 13:8; 17:8;
20:12, 15; 21:27). John is saying, "Do not miss anyone in sending our greetings" — **Greet the friends there by name!**

APPENDIX

STUDY QUESTIONS ON
FIRST, SECOND, AND THIRD JOHN

QUESTIONS ON FIRST JOHN

Consider These as You Read 1 John 1:1-4

1. Is there "scientific" proof for the truth of the Christian gospel?
2. What does the use of the verbs of hearing, seeing, and handling indicate about the author's relationship to the incarnation?
3. What does John say is his two-fold purpose of writing (1 John 1:3-4)?
4. How does John's claim to sensory experience with the "word of life" answer the *Gnostic problem?*
5. What other New Testament writing begins with a similar prologue?
6. What do we know about the word (logos) from John's Gospel? (Read John 1:1-14.)
7. How does this writing become part of the fulfillment of John's Apostolic Commission? (Compare 1 John 1:2-3 and Acts 1:8.)

Questions for Review of 1 John 1:1-4

1. How are John's answers to the Gnostic problem relevant in our time?

2. What does "God In A Test Tube" mean? In what way does the experience of John with the Incarnate Word prove the fact of God's being? (See John 14:1-9.)

3. Whom among the twelve Apostles demanded "scientific proof" of the resurrection? (See John 20:24-25.)

4. Why does John say "That which" rather than "Whom" in 1 John 1:1?

5. Name some specific incidents in the life of Jesus which John could still see "in his mind's eye."

6. What specific incidents in John's relationship with Jesus gave him opportunity to actually touch him?

7. What are John's qualifications to write this message?

8. What difference does the Incarnation make in the means by which we may understand life?

9. What is the key word of 1 John?

10. What is the real meaning of the word "fellowship" as used by the New Testament writers?

11. With whom do we have fellowship on the basis of the Apostolic witness to the Incarnation according to 1 John 1:3?

12. Does John write to bring people into the fellowship or to maintain those who are already in it?

13. What does the meaning of fellowship teach us about the necessity of the incarnation? (Cf. Hebrews 2:14-18.)

14. In addition to his concern that his readers remain in the fellowship of the Father and the Son, what is John's personal reason for this writing?

Consider These as You Read 1 John 1:5

1. Why does John change from the neuter "that which" of the prologue to the masculine "him?"

2. What does John mean by "light?"

3. What does John mean by "darkness?"

4. What are the practical implications of this verse for the Christian life?

Questions for Review of 1 John 1:5

1. What is the basis of John's argument in 1 John?
2. What statement by John summarizes the entire ministry of Jesus, including both his actions and teachings?
3. Describe the glory of God. (Read Exodus 24:17; 40:34 and 1 Kings 8:11.)
4. What did the oriental mystery cults teach about light and darkness?
5. What did the Greek and Roman religions teach about light and darkness?
6. When John says "God is light," does he agree or disagree with the pagan religions of the day? Explain.
7. What three "tests of life" constitute the framework of 1 John?
8. What does the light of God reveal about personal sin?
9. What is love in John's writings? What does love give and why?
10. How does John know God is light?
11. How does the truth revealed by Jesus differ from truth in other areas of investigation? How is it similar?
12. What gives meaning to truth discovered by man in the areas of science and the humanities?

Consider These as You Read 1 John 1:6-7

1. How is it possible for sinful men to "walk in the light as he is in the light?"
2. Why does John say ". . . we do not live by the truth," instead of saying ". . . we are not telling the truth?"
3. Why does John change from ". . . have fellowship with him" in verse 6 to ". . . have fellowship one with another . . ." in verse 7?

Questions for Review of 1 John 1:6-7

1. What are two practical results of walking in the light as he is in the light?
2. How does the light of God come into our lives?
3. Why do men refuse to walk in this light (John 3:16-21)?
4. How is the same truth contrasted in these two verses?
5. Does "walking in the light" imply moral perfection equal to that of God? Explain.
6. How is the truth of 1 John 1:6 related to that of John 14:6?
7. To walk in the light as he is in the light is to _____ .
8. What does God's light in Christ reveal about personal guilt?
9. Why are men at war with one another?
10. To leave the fellowship of those who walk in the light results in broken fellowship also with _____ .
11. The first thing the gospel message says to anyone is what?
12. How does the life of Jesus reveal the guilt of others?
13. What purifies us from all sin?
14. What is meant by the statement, "Nothing could be more diametrically opposed to the Gnostic than John's statement about the blood?" How is this the most "anti-Gnostic" terminology possible?
15. How is the summary statement of 1 John 1:6-7 relevant to the religious atmosphere of our day?

Consider These as You Read 1 John 1:8- 2:6

1. Is it possible for a child of God to sin?
2. What should a Christian do if he does sin?
3. What are the consequences of claiming we do not sin?
4. What is the relationship of Jesus *now* to a Christian who does sin?

5. What does it mean to "know" God?
6. Does the claim to know God in any way obligate the one making the claim?
7. What is the intended end of God's love to man?

Questions for Review of 1 John 1:8-2:6

1. What does the claim not to sin reveal about the sincerity of the one making the claim (1 John 1:8)?
2. What does "if we confess our sins" mean (1 John 1:9)?
3. What is the attitude toward God of one who claims he has not sinned (1 John 1:10)?
4. Why does John say he is writing these things (1 John 2:1)?
5. If one should sin, we have an advocate with the Father (1 John 2:1). Explain.
6. Jesus is our propitiation for our sin (1 John 2:2). Explain.
7. In what sense is Jesus also a propitiation for the sins of the whole world (1 John 2:2; compare 1 John 2:5)?
8. How does 1 John 2:3 challenge the claim of the Gnostic to special knowledge of God?
9. How is keeping God's commands evidence that we know him (1 John 2:4)?
10. How does the love of God reach its intended end in the life of the individual believer (1 John 2:5)?
11. What does it mean to "walk as Jesus walked" (1 John 2:6)?
12. What is the moral obligation of one who claims to know God (1 John 2:6)?
13. State in your own words, in a single sentence, the first test presented in 1 John whereby we may assure ourselves that we have eternal life.

Consider These as You Read 1 John 2:7-17

1. The relationship between spiritual darkness and hatred.
2. The relationship between light and love.

3. How a command can be both new and old.

4. How our relationship to our brothers in Christ indicates our relationship to God.

5. How the proper direction of love is essential to life.

6. Why one cannot love God and the world at once.

Questions for Review of 1 John 2:7-17

1. 1 John 2:7-11
   a. To what command does John refer in vv. 7 & 8?
   b. How can this command be both new and old?
   c. What is the significance of "Dear friends" in v. 7?
   d. Explain why John here commands to love our brothers rather than our enemies. (Compare v. 5.)
   e. What is the source of brotherhood?
   f. How is the absence of love proof that one is "walking in darkness?"
   g. What are two possible interpretations of v. 10?
   h. Which of these two seems most likely to be John's real meaning? Support your answer.

2. 1 John 2:12-14
   a. What is one possible explanation of John's repetition in these verses?
   b. Of what blessing is the new Christian likely to be most aware?
   c. What is the significance of John's writing to the older men of the church "because you have known him who is from the beginning?"
   d. Why does John address the young men, "Because you are strong, and the word of God lives in you, and you have overcome the evil one?"

3. 1 John 2:15-17
   a. What is the meaning of "love" as John uses it here?
   b. What is the basis for the conclusion, "Man must love something?"
   c. What three classifications does John use for the "things of the world?"

d. What is the meaning of "the cravings of sinful man" (v. 16)?

e. What is the meaning of "the lust of his eyes?"

f. What is the meaning of "boasting of what he has and does?"

g. If there is nothing essentially wrong with these things, why does John demand that we not love them?

h. What is the result of loving God?

i. What is the result of loving the things of the world?

j. How does the statement that a Christian has "passed away" reflect fuzzy thinking about the results of love?

Consider These as You Read 1 John 2:18-28

1. How our faith in Jesus as God's only Son is evidence that we are in fellowship with God.

2. What is the meaning of antichrist?

3. What does our anointing from the Holy Spirit have to do with the truth that Jesus is the Christ?

4. Who are those who "went out from us?"

5. How does the promise of eternal life relate to our holding fast the message of the gospel?

6. How does being mindful of our anointing keep us from denying Jesus?

Questions for Review of 1 John 2:18-28

1. What is the significance of the fact that there is no "the" with last hour (v. 18)?

2. What is the purpose of 1 John?

3. What do the terms "last hour" and "last day" seem to indicate in pre-Christian usage?

4. In what sense may the entire Christian era be considered a last hour?

5. What light do Acts 2:16ff and Galatians 3:6-29 throw on John's discussion of a last hour in connection with the Christian's anointing of the Holy Spirit?

6. What is the literal meaning of the word "Christ?"

7. If one is against Christ, is he not opposed to all those who are anointed of God?

8. Who, besides Jesus, may be called "anointed ones?"

9. Does the Bible anywhere identify antichrist with the "Man of Sin?"

10. If the coming of Christ is the beginning of a last hour, is not the coming of those who oppose him and his anointed ones also proof of the same?

11. Are there antichrists in the world today? Explain.

12. What proves that the antichrists were not "of us" (v. 19)?

13. What is the relationship of the church to the presence of Christ on earth today (v. 20)?

14. Who receives the anointing of the Holy Spirit?

15. Is "scholarship" to be feared by the uneducated Christian? Explain (v. 21).

16. What is the decisive proof of falsehood (vv. 22-23)?

17. Can one claim honestly to know God as Father while denying the deity of Jesus?

18. Who first presented the idea that God is Father?

19. What is the condition of eternal life presented by John in this passage (vv. 24-25)?

20. What is the standard by which all truth is determined?

21. What is the relationship between knowledge of God and presence of eternal life?

22. How does the awareness of the presence of the Holy Spirit make the denial of Christ less likely?

23. Who has most reason to be afraid and ashamed in the presence of Jesus (v. 28)?

Consider These as You Read 1 John 2:29

1. The meaning of righteous and righteousness.
2. The relationship of divine sonship to personal righteousness in terms of cause and effect.
3. How righteousness is an unavoidable test of truth for the claim to be a son of God.

Questions for Review of 1 John 2:29

1. In the first cycle of tests presented in 1 John, the author tests fellowship with God as _____ .
2. In the present cycle of tests, introduced in 1 John 2:29, he tests fellowship with God as _____ .
3. In testing fellowship as walking in the light, the proof lies in our _____ .
4. In testing fellowship as divine sonship, the proof lies in our outward _____ .
5. The outward test of personal righteousness corresponds to our attitude toward _____ .
6. The outward test of behavior toward our brothers corresponds to our inward attitude of _____ for them.
7. Our open confession of Jesus as the Christ corresponds to our inward _____ .
8. In 1 John 2:29, the idea of _____ is introduced for the first time in 1 John.
9. What is the proof presented in 1 John 2:29 as the natural result of having been born of God?
10. What is the meaning of righteousness as used in this verse?
11. What is the difference between the righteousness practiced by the sons of God and the subjective "goodness" of the "new morality?"

Consider These as You Read 1 John 3:1-3

1. What "manner of love" has God shown us?

2. Why does the world not know the sons of God?

3. How will "seeing him as he is" transform us to become like him?

Questions for Review of 1 John 3:1-3

1. Compare 1 John 3:1 with John 3:16.

2. Eternal life, here tested as divine sonship, results from the same _____ .

3. Not just Calvary, but the entire _____ brought God's love to bear upon our need.

4. The contemporary countrymen of Jesus rejected him because they could not accept a _____ as God's Son.

5. The Gnostic could accept the humanity of Jesus without rejecting his _____ .

6. How does the modern "pseudo-intellectual" rejection of the deity of Jesus follow the same pattern as that of the Jews and the Gnostics?

7. What is John's constant reaction to the awareness that he is a son of God?

8. How is this amazement contrasted to the modern philosophy of the "fatherhood of God and brotherhood of man?"

9. Brotherhood results from common _____ .

10. To become a child of God one must _____ (John 1:12).

11. When does eternal life begin?

12. When do we begin to be the sons of God?

13. What light does 1 Corinthians 15:35 shed on 1 John 3:2?

14. How does the awareness of present sonship and future glory affect the lives of the children of God?

15. Is one a child of God because he is righteous, or is righteousness the result of divine sonship?

Consider These as You Read 1 John 3:4-10

1. If we are not under law, how is sin considered lawlessness?
2. Is it impossible for a child of God to sin?
3. How does the "seed" of God remain in the child of God?
4. Who are the children of the devil?
5. What is the basic moral contrast between the life of sin and the life of divine Sonship?

Questions for Review of 1 John 3:4-10

1. All sin is contrary to God's authority. Explain.
2. God's original plan was to have a family of children who were _____ and without _____ (Ephesians 1:4).
3. To be without blemish is to be _____ as a result of holiness.
4. The opposite of holiness is _____ .
5. Lawlessness always results in _____ behavior.
6. What is the difference between paternity and fatherhood?
7. The purpose for which Christ came is stated two ways in this passage. What are they?
8. Who was originally responsible for the accomplishment of God's purpose in man?
9. How does the character of Jesus demonstrate the need for righteousness in the lives of God's children?
10. What is the secret of Jesus' sinless life?
11. Total commitment always issues in a _____ life.
12. What does John mean by "remaining in him?"
13. Righteousness to John is not theory but _____ .
14. What is the origin of all sin?
15. Does the Bible attempt to prove there is a devil?

16. What is the basis upon which Jesus said some are children of the devil (John 8:44)?

17. What is the origin of righteousness?

Consider These as You Read 1 John 3:11-24

1. What is the relation of command to love (3:11) and to God as light (1:5) since both are presented as summary of the divine message?

2. How does the first murder demonstrate the effect of hate on the one hating?

3. Can a Christian ever be liked by the world? Explain. (Compare 1 John 3:13 and Acts 2:47.)

4. When do Christians pass from death to life?

5. How can one be a murderer without killing anyone?

6. What is the relationship of love to need?

7. How do one's actions prove or disprove one's claim to divine sonship?

8. Should a Christian ever feel guilty to the point of self-condemnation?

9. Why are so many prayers seemingly unanswered?

10. What is Christian behavior in matters where there is no express command from God?

11. How does the experience of answered prayer have any bearing on John's argument that Jesus is indeed the Christ?

12. How does the habit of believing Christ and loving our brothers affirm the deity of Christ?

13. How does the presence of the Holy Spirit in our lives affirm the deity of Christ?

Questions for Review of 1 John 3:11-24

1. The second summary of the message of the incarnation in 1 John 3:11 is _____.

2. It is the nature of the life which we have in Christ to become a source of _____ to others.
3. This is accomplished when we _____ .
4. How does the murder of Abel by Cain demonstrate that the world is prone to hate those who practice righteousness?
5. The confrontation of righteousness by unrighteousness *normally* results in _____ .
6. Because love is obedience to God it is also _____ .
7. When does a Christian "pass from death to life?"
8. Do we love because we have eternal life, or do we have eternal life because we love?
9. Hate is the absence of _____ just as _____ is the absence of light.
10. The word translated "hate" in 1 John 3:15 means _____ .
11. Failure to love is proof of the absence of _____ .
12. How does the world become aware of love as we know it in Christ?
13. How do we demonstrate divine love in such a way that it is recognizable?
14. Just as he brought eternal life in the presence of our need, so we are to give in the presence of temporal needs.
15. Does giving what we can afford demonstrate divine love? Explain.
16. Many will be surprised in the judgment, who expect to be saved, because they have not learned to give rather than _____ .
17. How may we have assurance before God, even when our hearts condemn us?
18. Explain the statement, "No Christian has any right to a guilt complex."

19. One of the greatest blessings of the Christian life is realized forgiveness. Explain this statement in light of 1 John 3:20.

20. The only basis upon which one's heart can fail to condemn him is _____ .

21. The experience of answered prayer is evidence of _____ according to 1 John 3:22.

22. What conditions must be present in our lives in order to pray effectively?

23. Why does the term "father" not suggest authority to us today?

24. Which is more important, the question, "Who is Jesus?" Or our personal belief in the answer, "You are the Christ, the Son of the Living God?"

25. _____ is still the only hope of healing the divisions caused by false teaching.

26. How does the anointing of the Spirit demonstrate that we are in the Christ?

Consider These as You Read 1 John 4:1-6

1 How does the presence of the Spirit prove we have been born of God?

2. Are there preachers (or prophets) who deliberately and knowingly preach what they know to be false?

3. Are men today as conscious of the "spirit world" as they were in the first century?

4. Is the Spirit not as active in the church today as in John's time?

5. When one denies Jesus as Christ, what is he actually denying?

6. Why will false teachers not listen to truth?

7. If people have a faulty concept of life and reality, are they beyond the preaching of the gospel to them is useless?

Questions for Review of 1 John 4:1-6

1. What is the meaning of the phrase "of God" or "from God" as used in this passage of 1 John ?
2. At what point does Christian tolerance become gullibility?
3. How do you account for the fact that the outward demonstration of the Spirit was more evident in the first century church than today?
4. What is the test by which we are to "prove the spirits to see whether they are of God?"
5. What is the primary work of a prophet?
6. Why do prophets often refer to future events in revealing the present will of God?
7. What does John's test prove about the claim of modern liberals that the Ecumenical Movement is led by the Spirit of God? Explain.
8. Does the *fact* of spiritual activity prove that the activity originates in God? What is the test of divine origin for such activity?
9. To recognize Jesus as Messiah is to recognize him as _____ and _____ .
10. As Prophet, how does the Christ function?
11. As Priest, how does the Christ function?
12. As King, how does the Christ function?
13. What is the difference between confessing that Jesus as Christ came as flesh and confessing simply that Jesus is the Christ?
14. The man, Jesus, whom we confess as Christ, is not of human origin. Explain.
15. John 1:1 teaches three things about Jesus that have a direct bearing on the confession here presented as a test of false teaching. What are those three things?
16. In order to accomplish the purpose of God in man, Jesus _____ with his own blood.

17. To do this he became flesh, thus _____ with those he came to redeem.

18. It is in the capacity of divine Redeemer that he voluntarily submitted himself to learn _____ .

19. To be recognized as originating in God, to be Christian, the message of a prophet must _____ .

20. Why does John refer to the spirit of antichrist as "it" rather than "he?"

21. What is meant by the statement, "The children of God have the assistance of God himself . . . whereas the false prophets are "on their own?"

Consider These as You Read 1 John 4:7-12

1. How can John say "everyone who loves has been born of God," and then refer to Jesus as "his one and only Son?"

2. How is the practice of loving evidence of knowing God?

3. How can John say "God is light" (1 John 1:5) and then say "God is love" in this passage?

4. How is God's love for us related to our loving one another?

5. What is the end perfection of God's love?

Questions for Review of 1 John 4:7-12

1. Why does John say we are to love one another?

2. What is the source of Christian love?

3. God learned what it is like to be human through _____ .

4. The experience by which we get to know "what it is like to be God" is the experience of _____ .

5. Name experiences that are common to both God and man.

6. Loving your brothers proves that we are _____ .

7. Does John say that love is God? Explain.

8. What evidence is there in 1 John 4:9-10 that John is familiar with the virgin birth of Jesus?

9. Jesus is God's Son by _____ while we may become God's sons through _____ .

10. How do you reconcile the claim "Jesus is God as man" with the statement, "Jehovah, he is God, there is none other than he alone?"

11. The term "Son of God" applied to Jesus describes _____ .

12. Why did Jesus become a man?

13. What is the only way in which God can become a man and still be God?

14. Our acceptance of God's love for us carries with it the moral obligation to _____ .

15. One who does not love has no _____ .

16. The love of God reaches its intended end when God _____ .

17. Evidence of God in us is that we _____ .

18. The ultimate knowledge that man can have of God comes from the experience of _____ .

Consider These as You Read 1 John 4:13-16

1. How the Spirit of God in us is evidence that we are in him and he in us.

2. The significance of John's reference here to his eyewitness experience with Jesus.

3. How confession of Jesus as the Son of God is evidence we are in God and God in us.

4. How love can be the object of belief.

5. Why John repeats here what he has already said in 1 John 4:8, that "God is love."

Questions for Review of 1 John 4:13-16

1. What are two alternatives concerning John's reference in v. 13 to "the Spirit he has given us?"
2. What is the essential testimony of the Spirit?
3. To what does John appeal in v. 14 as the basis of his claim that Jesus is God's Son and the Savior of the world?
4. What are the tests by which phenomena of the past are established as historical?
5. How does the resurrection prove the claim of Jesus to be the Son of God and Savior of the world?
6. Does the resurrection, as recorded in the New Testament, meet the tests of historicity? Explain your answer.
7. Can you suggest other events in the life of Jesus which may be put to the same test?
8. What is meant by "the area where the experience of God and the experience of man merge?"
9. The love which we share with God was first brought to light by _____ .
10. In what way is the love of God said to be the object of the Christian's faith?
11. Is John here discussing the means by which we come to salvation? Explain your answer.
12. Can the "steps to salvation" contradict the evidences that we are indeed in a saving relationship to God? Explain.

Consider These as You Read 1 John 4:17–5:3

1. What is the relationship of obedience to righteousness?
2. What is the relationship of righteousness to love?
3. Why do Christians love their brothers in Christ?
4. Who is my brother in Christ?
5. How may I know that I am fulfilling the command to love my brother?

Questions for Review of 1 John 4:17-5:3

1. How is righteousness said to be a demonstration of love?
2. What is the intended end of our love for our brothers?
3. Does one who loves his brother fear death? Explain.
4. Is the preaching of love "soft pedaling" the gospel? Explain.
5. What is the one command of God which cannot be counterfeited?
6. What is the difference between these two statements:
   (a) "I love him because he first loved me."
   (b) "I love because he first loved me?"
7. How can I identify my Christian brother? Explain.
8. Is there a difference between "being begotten" and "being born," in terms of entrance into the family of God?
9. Explain the meaning of "regeneration."
10. Explain why the teaching that baptism is essential to salvation is not the same as teaching salvation by works.
11. Faith is always _____ .
12. Divine love in God's children is not recognized by feeling but by _____ .
13. If we learn to love our brothers, and practice this love, we may even learn to _____ .
14. Explain how God's commands are not burdensome to one who loves him.

Consider These as You Read 1 John 5:4-12

1. What does John mean by "overcome the world?"
2. How does faith that Jesus is the Christ enable one to overcome the world?
3. How does the Spirit testify that Jesus is the Son of God?
4. What should be the Bible believer's attitude toward textual problems such as the one found in some versions of 1 John 5:7b?

5. What has God testified concerning his Son?

6. Is it possible to have eternal life and not believe that Jesus is indeed the Christ, the Son of God? Explain your answer.

7. Is it possible to not call Jesus "Lord" and have eternal life?

Questions for Review of 1 John 5:4-12

1. Why is the statement concerning the three witnesses which is found in the King James Version of 1 John omitted from more recent versions (v. 7)?

2. Why are the commands of God not burdensome to the children of God?

3. What is the source of victorious power in the life of a Christian which is not available to the world?

4. How does the life of the "average church member" today support the doctrine of Karl Marx that "religion is the opiate of the people?"

5. Give a definition of "faith" as John uses it in 1 John 5:4.

6. Explain the statement, "The sons of God are not the victims of circumstance."

7. Is faith just a positive attitude toward life?

8. One form of Gnosticism called Cerenthic claimed that whatever was divine about Jesus came upon him at _____ and left him at _____ .

9. What is John's answer to this claim?

10. The Spirit and the water and the blood all testify to one thing. What is the purpose of their testimony?

11. In our day, the testimony of the Spirit includes what?

12. How does the Spirit testify of Jesus' presence in our own lives?

13. In order for rationalism to destroy belief in the deity of Jesus it must first destroy the _____ of Scripture.

14. The person who does not believe in the deity of Jesus as the incarnate Son of God has made the Spirit a _____ .

15. Real victory over the world comes from faith which gives us a constant awareness of _____ .

16. A great deal of our failure to overcome the world comes from our inability to keep to _____ .

17. To have victory over the world is to make _____ the master and _____ the servant.

18. How does our giving to the church aid in our overcoming the world in our personal lives?

Consider These as You Read 1 John 5:13-21

1. How does one remove the "maybes" concerning his hope of eternal life?

2. What is the source of confidence in prayer?

3. If no one who is born of God sins, why does John ask that we pray for a brother when we see him sinning?

4. What is "the sin that leads to death?"

5. Does 1 John 5:18 support the doctrine of "eternal security?"

6. How is idolatry related to the danger of Gnosticism against which this letter was written?

Questions for Review of 1 John 5:13-21

1. In addition to our experience in Christian living, we also may rely upon _____ to confirm the certainty of eternal life.

2. What is John's reason for writing 1 John, as stated in his own words?

3. How does this reason for writing correspond with his reason for writing the fourth Gospel?

4. Can man ever cease to be created in the image of God? What meaning does this give to eternal life?

5. Eternal life is that *kind* of life that finds its fullest expression in _____ .

6. While life identified with this present world produces _____ , eternal life produces _____ . (Cf. Galatians 3:20-ff.)

7. Believing "into the name" of the Son of God means _____ .

8. Name five limitations which John places upon prayer.

9. What is the single exception to the certainty of prayer which meets these limitations?

10. Why does John discuss the certainty of prayer in this letter which deals with the evidences of eternal life?

11. What does the Bible teach about the "unpardonable sin?"

12. What does John mean by "sinning sin toward death?"

13. "Continuing to sin" describes a _____ rather than a _____ .

14. List three distinct certainties upon which the child of God can stake his eternal life.

15. What is meant by "understanding" in 1 John 5:20?

16. A Christian not only does his best to avoid sin, he relies upon _____ to make up the difference between what he does and what he ought to do.

17. How is the danger of idolatry even more dangerous now than when John wrote?

QUESTIONS ON SECOND JOHN

Consider These as You Read 2 John

1. Who is "the elder"?

2. Who is "the elect lady"?

3. Is there more to verse 3 than the mere formality of greeting?

4. Who are the children of verse 4?

5. What is the purpose of John's writing in 2 John?

6. Why is 2 John so short?

Questions for Review of 2 John

1. What are some of the different views of the identity of "the elect lady?"

2. What is the probable meaning of the term "elder" as used here by John?

3. Against what does 2 John constitute a warning (v. 8)?

4. How does John's position against Gnosticism answer the present day philosophy that "all truth is relative?"

5. Describe the grace of God.

6. Sin, in its deepest sense, is a crime against what or whom?

7. A crime against law can be punished by _____.

8. A crime against love can only be atoned for by _____.

9. How would you answer the claim that the peace of God in the heart of Christians is "the opiate of the people" to lull them into the grasp of those who would enslave and exploit?

10. Why is John pleasantly surprised to find the wandering children of the elect lady walking according to truth?

11. The only admissible evidence that we know truth is that we _____ (v. 4).

12. The fundamental command of God to his children is that we _____.

13. How does love express itself (v. 6)?

14. Love will not allow _____ with falsehood.

15. Who does John identify as the antichrist in 2 John? How does this compare with what John says about the antichrist in 1 John, chapter 2?

16. The essential truth upon which both the personal salvation of Christians and the fellowship of the church rests is _____ .

17. What is meant by "the teaching of Christ" in 2 John 9?

18. What is the danger of "progress" as set forth in 2 John 9?

19. Why are we forbidden to be hospitable to false teachers?

20. How would a Christian share in wickedness (v. 11)?

21. Who might be chosen sister be?

QUESTIONS ON THIRD JOHN

Consider These as You Read 3 John

1. Why did John write to Gaius?

2. Is there any gnostic influence here as in 1 and 2 John?

3. What part does Diotrephes play in the problem?

4. Why is Demetrius mentioned?

Questions for Review of 3 John

1. What significance do you attach to John's repeated referral to Gaius as "friend?"

2. What position did Gaius probably hold in his home congregation?

3. What is the problem about which John writes Gaius (vv. 10,11)?

4. Contrast the personality of Gaius with that of Diotrephes.

5. What treatment does John ask of Gaius for the visiting ministers?

6. What is the significance of the term "send them on their way?"

7. Why on a mission field might it be wise not to take money from those to whom the gospel is preached?

8. What is the reward promised by John to those who support the preachers of the gospel?

9. What wrong had Diotrephes done?

10. What damage is possible to the church when an elder accuses a minister "by gossiping maliciously?"

11. How do genuine Christians often imitate evil men such as Diotrephes?

12. What are two possible identifications for Demetrius?

13. What three witnesses to the genuineness of Demetrius does John name?